Best Wishes,

Kerry Senn

PRAISE FOR *The Ownership Mindset*

"If you are looking for a great book that shows exactly what impact creating a culture of empowering employees to be owners can have on an organization, *The Ownership Mindset* is it. Kerry Siggins is an inspiring leader that we all can learn from."

KARA GOLDIN, founder and CEO, Hint Water, and author of the *Wall Street Journal* bestseller *Undaunted*

"Kerry has written a compelling, entertaining, and inspiring story of what it takes to go from rock bottom to an influential leader and industry disruptor. *The Ownership Mindset* is essential for any leader who doesn't believe that being vulnerable, authentic, and employee-centric creates success. Kerry is clearly on the consistent, persistent pursuit of her potential!"

DAVID MELTZER, founder, David Meltzer Enterprises and Sports 1 Marketing

"In this powerful and introspective book, Kerry Siggins offers a bold vision that inspires teams and individuals to play offense in highly defensive environments by thinking like an owner at scale. *The Ownership Mindset* is a fascinating combination of heartful conviction and practical advice you can immediately put into action. It lays out a compelling message: own your purpose, own your leadership, own your life."

PAUL EPSTEIN, former NFL and NBA executive and bestselling author of *The Power of Playing Offense*

"Ownership is a core value of the up-and-coming generations in the workforce. Kerry is at the forefront of a new breed of innovative leaders who are making their mark by embracing this fact as more than a slogan. *The Ownership Mindset* is the must-read handbook for creating and sustaining positive, lasting change in the radically new world of work."

SANTOR NISHIZAKI, leadership expert and co-author of *Working with Gen Z*

"Kerry Siggins doesn't just talk about an ownership mindset, she shows you how to confidently live and lead with it through her vulnerable stories and incredible journey from rock bottom to CEO. This book is perfect for leaders who want to use practical strategies to lead themselves and others in a results-driven way."

KELLI THOMPSON, award-winning career and leadership coach; author of *Closing the Confidence Gap*

"A leadership book isn't supposed to be this real, raw, and heartfelt. But that's who Kerry is. It's also chock-full of actionable advice for everyone from founders to the entry-level on every page about how to achieve a better version of yourself and your team."

FRANKIE RUSSO, eight-time *Inc.* 500 entrepreneur and bestselling author of *Breaking WHY*

"Kerry Siggins has a way of captivating you from the get-go with her story of overcoming addiction to lead a dynamic and disruptive company. I showcased Kerry on my podcast, *Creating Confidence*, and the response was overwhelming! Her story and direction not only inspire but also advise and direct others to a path of fulfillment and success. *The Ownership Mindset* is a handbook for all leaders who want to build a high-performing culture where employees love what they do. Take direction from someone who has been where you want to go. Kerry's book is your roadmap to success."

HEATHER MONAHAN, bestselling author of *Confidence Creator* and keynote speaker

"An ownership mindset is crucial to breathing life into organizations of all shapes and sizes. Kerry's book puts this important truth front and center while providing powerful inspiration and a deep well of user-friendly wisdom to which you'll return again and again."

JASON BARGER, award-winning leadership consultant and author of *Breathing Oxygen*

an imprint of Amplify Publishing Group

www.amplifypublishinggroup.com

The Ownership Mindset:
A Handbook for Transforming Your Life and Leadership

For more information, please contact:
Amplify Publishing, an imprint of Amplify Publishing Group
620 Herndon Parkway, Suite 320
Herndon, VA 20170
info@amplifypublishing.com

Library of Congress Control Number: 2023900411

CPSIA Code: PRV0223A

ISBN-13: 978-1-63755-434-0

Printed in the United States

To the past, present, and future
StoneAge employees
who are Owning It every day.
You make leading worthwhile.

THE
OWNER-
SHIP
MIND-
SET

A Handbook for Transforming Your Life and Leadership

KERRY SIGGINS

an imprint of Amplify Publishing Group

CONTENTS

PART THREE
LEADING OTHERS

INTRODUCTION

When I am asked when it was that I knew I was a leader, I say I came out of the womb that way. My mom teased me, saying that I was the boss of the family by the time I was five years old. I have always had the knack to make things happen, to manifest my desires—or as my brother would put it: *I always got my way*. I knew what I wanted and could communicate my wants and needs; therefore, I made it easy for others to say yes. Some might call this manipulation, but I call it a unique ability to influence.

There are so many attributes that go into being an exceptional leader. Knowing where you want to go (vision) and how to motivate in a way that brings others along, or better yet, *inspires* them to help you achieve your vision (influence) are fundamental to leadership.

Exceptional leaders understand that true ownership is fully owning everything that happens in your life. It means you understand you are responsible for your attitude, actions, reactions, teamwork, communication, and relationships. It also means you hold others accountable for their commitments and contributions. I refuse to play a victim, and I have adopted the mindset that things don't happen *to* me, they happen *because* of me.

I have carried this mindset of ownership forward, and it is a cornerstone in all that I do and all that happens at StoneAge—a company that offers its employees literal ownership through an Employee Stock Ownership Program (ESOP).

I wrote this book for first-time CEOs, founders, entrepreneurs, and executives—those looking to become exceptional leaders but aren't sure how to navigate the intricacies of being in the C-suite, especially as a CEO. It's for those newly appointed CEOs, executives, or first-time founders seeking guidance, inspiration, and advice. I am hopeful that you can learn from my missteps and mistakes and my wins and successes. I share my story from a place of vulnerability and transparency, giving you the raw truth of what it's like to learn how to be a CEO.

For the more seasoned CEO, executive, and entrepreneur, this book can serve as a reminder on how to show up, do the work, and make an impact. Many of us lose sight of why we chose to become leaders from time to time, and I hope that my stories and examples can reinspire even the most tenured CEO and executives to step up and show up with authenticity, vulnerability, and grit.

I might know what you are thinking, and I get it. There are thousands of leadership books out there. Why is this one different? Why should I read this book?

No leadership journey is the same. There is no one way to lead, no one way to build a lasting company. What makes each leadership journey unique is the story. And my story takes me from hitting rock bottom due to substance abuse to running an innovative and disruptive company, and—at the risk of not sounding humble—it's also a model for leaders of all sorts.

You see, I believe that business leaders can change the world. Not only can they, but they also have an obligation to do so. We business leaders have a responsibility to leave this world a better place, and we can do this by recognizing that every person in our organization matters.

Leaders of today and those who lead in the future will change the world because they will be stewards of their employees. They know that by respecting all people for their work effort, dignity, intelligence, and overall humanity, they can create lasting organizations that make communities, countries, and continents better places—if they take full ownership.

These game-changing leaders believe the economy is built from the middle out and therefore pay livable wages and share in the company's success. These exceptional leaders know they must eradicate the premise that the purpose of companies is to maximize shareholder returns and instead focus their efforts on improving the lives and livelihoods of their employees and customers.

I am meeting my obligation of leaving the world a better place by telling my story and providing a framework for developing deep personal responsibility as a person and a leader. Surviving an overdose crystalized the power of cultivating an ownership mindset. Through the power of responsibility and accountability, we all can make the world a better place. I am living proof if it.

In this book, I'll invite you to join my journey to becoming one of these leaders and offer advice and observations on why the ownership mindset is a powerful tool and how you can use it to help you on your own path.

Thank you for sharing this journey with me. Now let's get started.

PART ONE
TAKING OWNERSHIP

1

A CRASH COURSE

When I was a child, I loved Dr. Seuss, despite his adverse qualities. His books were funny, silly, and made me think. *Do I like green eggs and ham? Or do I hate them, just like Sam?* Earnest questions to contemplate when you are eight years old. But even as an adult, I enjoy his stories.

There is one book in particular that resonates with the way I live my life. *Oh, the Places You'll Go!* is filled with twists and turns and has a message that we all can live by. The book starts like this: "Congratulations, today is your day. You're off to great places. You're off and away. You have brains in your head. You have feet in your shoes. You can steer yourself in any direction you choose."

Those are powerful words.

"You can steer yourself in any direction you choose."

One beautiful thing about being human is that every day we get to choose. Choose what time we get out of bed. Choose what we are going to wear. Choose whom we want to marry or if we don't want to marry at all. Choose to be happy or angry or sad. And we choose what we say and how we will react to all the good things and bad things that happen in life. Life is filled with choices, and it's our responsibility to own them. To own our responses. To own our actions.

When I was in ninth grade, I had an English teacher whom I couldn't stand. In my wise and accurate fourteen-year-old opinion, he was arrogant, condescending, and a terrible teacher. Therefore, I used it as an excuse to blow him off, disrupt class, and complain about him frequently. One day, he announced that we would write reports, and he permitted us to write on any topic we chose. Because I loved pushing my boundaries and I wanted to aggravate him, I chose the topic of contraceptive options. Apparently, he didn't think this was appropriate for a ninth-grade report, so he called my mom to discuss my behavior and choice. My mom told him that she approved of my decision to write about contraceptive options. He had, after all, given us the freedom to choose whatever topic we wanted. My mom suggested that he talk to me directly about why I was being such a pain in his class. I had listened to the entire conversation because, back then, we used landlines, and I was a pro at picking up the phone without anyone knowing.

"MOM!!! I can't believe you just did that. I don't want to talk to him," I snapped at her after we both hung up the phones. I was so angry; I wanted her to tell him that he was a terrible teacher and to stop trying to make an example of me. I wanted her to fix my problem. But she didn't. She smiled calmly and said, "Welcome to this thing called life. You purposefully chose that topic to make him mad, and now you get to deal with the consequences of that choice."

The next day, Mr. Statton pulled me aside and asked me to meet at 3:30 p.m. We sat at a picnic bench outside of the main school entrance. I'll never forget my classmates streaming by, giggling and whispering about why I was sitting after school talking to a teacher. I was embarrassed and wanted to run. *Oh god*, I thought. *They are going to think I am such a loser. Or in trouble. Ugh.*

But I didn't run; I didn't have the guts to walk away. Partly because I knew I was in the wrong. And partly because I didn't want to get in trouble. And mostly, deep down, I wanted Mr. Statton to think I was a good student.

Then something amazing happened. We actually started to have a conversation. A good conversation. I told him how I felt about his class and the way he talked to us. I told him I felt dismissed and that he was condescending. He told me that he thought I was squandering a golden opportunity to learn and to become a better writer. He told me that I was wasting my leadership skills by misbehaving and by setting a poor example. By the end of the meeting, we both apologized for our actions and how we treated each other. We both agreed to do better. And he let me write my report on contraceptive options, which I did, and it turned out to be a great educational opportunity—in more ways than one.

What I didn't realize that day was how profound this experience would be. The confidence I gained changed the course of my life forever. I learned the power of facing conflict head-on, advocating for myself, and taking feedback even when it was tough to hear. I learned how being accountable not only for my actions but also for how I engage in challenging conversations empowered me to make different choices in my life. I learned not to be a victim of my circumstance; instead, I saw a way to change my circumstance to make my life better—starting with taking ownership of the situation I found myself in.

We complicated beings are merely a collection of all the individual moments in our lives and the stories we tell ourselves about these moments. This early high school moment stands out because it changed my story, my narrative about how someone else needs to solve my problems *for* me. No! I can solve my own problems! I can take responsibility for my actions as well as the outcomes of my decisions and responses.

I needed to learn to own my life.

In my late twenties, this lesson would once again prove valuable.

• • •

It has been said that people will work for money, but they will die for recognition. I know a thing or two about that. It's a basic human desire to want to be recognized for our inherent value. Leaders are no different. In fact, for many of us, the desire to be recognized is a motivator, pushing us to be impactful. But this widely held desire can also be dangerous for leaders. It can cause you to deflect, blame, lie, and distort—all of which are the exact opposite of the ownership mindset.

The need to be recognized and acknowledged is a deep part of my personality. My personality is driven by wanting to be seen. Seen as successful. Seen as talented. Seen as smart. Seen as an exceptional leader. When your ego drives everything you do, you often forget that the world doesn't revolve around you. And when the ego goes unchecked, it can also result in your destruction.

I used to think the secret to success was hard work. I used to believe that it was about being smart and talented. Success meant being better than everyone else. As long as I was being recognized, I would go far. And this mindset of *me first, everyone else second* almost destroyed me. I didn't understand what it meant to have an ownership mindset. Truth be told, you would often find me attempting to justify my self-centeredness or deflecting mistakes.

Looking back, after hundreds of hours of therapy, coaching, and deep self-exploration, I better understand why my deep need to be seen and recognized drove me to self-sabotage. My father left when I was a young child, and even though my mother loved me deeply and provided a remarkable life for my brother and me, I felt abandoned and unseen by my dad. Internally, I questioned, *Why doesn't he love me? What do I have to do to prove myself? What do I have to do to make him see me?* I don't blame my dad for my problems, and I no longer carry anger or resentment toward him. I understand that he was dealing with his own demons, too.

At the time, the combination of my high-achiever personality style, need for recognition, and feeling unloved by my father made me feel lonely and powerless. The only way I knew how to fill this void was to vie for attention. The need to be seen as worthy manifested itself in many negative ways—lying for attention, overstating my capabilities, and pushing boundaries to make others notice me. I did many stupid things as an adolescent and teen, including stealing and wrecking my grandfather's truck, dating guys much older than me, selling weed and mushrooms to my friends, and skipping school regularly.

In my twenties, these patterns drove me to prove that I could get the best drugs in Austin and do more cocaine than a 230-pound man. A worthy goal, no doubt. But I also would never admit that I was a high-functioning addict; instead, I talked about my friends' and coworkers' drug problems behind their backs. I always went to work, no matter how messed up I was. And I manipulated situations to get attention and to get what I wanted: a feeling of success.

In fact, I worked with one of my friends who was in serious trouble with drugs, and she started to lie to me about how bad it was. I began to obsess over her lies and make her out to be a bad person, a bad friend, and a bad colleague. She missed work over and over, and I judged her for it. My rule: party hard, work hard. *She should still be coming to work,* I told myself. But if I am honest, I was secretly happy she was failing at work. I was hoping to win salesperson of the year, and the worse she performed, the better I would measure up. My boss, frustrated with her, asked me what was going on, and I told her. My friend got fired, and I got a promotion. Even though I felt remorseful and guilty after the words came out of my mouth, I justified it. *It's her problem. She's the one who didn't go to work. She's the one who failed*, I told myself. Not my proudest moment.

In 2006, the tables turned.

I overdosed. By myself, on the floor of my apartment. I nursed myself through the overdose; there was no way I was calling for help. I couldn't allow anyone to see me in this state. My ego couldn't handle it. Luckily, I didn't die. I don't know how I didn't.

As I lay there on the floor, all I could think about was the state of my relationships.

I thought back to all the people I hurt, dismissed, gossiped about, judged, stepped on, and ignored. I thought about how I had been pretending to be someone I wasn't.

I thought about how selfish I was and how my ego controlled me. I questioned why I pushed boundaries and why I wanted so damn badly to be seen. I was filled with shame and regret.

I missed work three days in a row, and none of my friends or coworkers called to check on me. I realized that for all the effort I put into being popular, trendy, and successful, hardly anyone cared that much about me. Not unless I was partying with them at the club or helping them achieve their goals at the office. I wasn't a leader. I didn't have many real friends. I lived beyond my means and filled my closet with clothes I couldn't afford. In my garage sat a sports car that I struggled to make payments on. I wasn't the image I was trying to portray. Not even close. I was a lonely human being using substances to create an alternate reality, one where I didn't feel so alone and inadequate. I was an utter disappointment.

When I finally mustered enough strength to take a shower, I looked in the mirror and broke down. Enough was enough was enough. I knew

I had potential and could live a more fulfilling, successful life. I knew deep down that I was failing. Failing at work, failing in my relationships, failing in my life. I didn't want to live this way, and I needed help. I looked in the mirror and said:

"Today is the today you stop lying to yourself and to everyone else. Today is the day that you start to value relationships and hold yourself accountable. Today, you will stop letting your ego drive you, and you will fix the mess you've made. Today is the day that you change your life forever."

And then I cried. *Where do I start?* I thought.

With a true friend, I heard my higher self respond softly.

There was one person in my life at the time, besides my mother, whom I had invested effort into building a relationship with—Joe.

Joe was not your average friend. He wasn't a party friend. I met him through work, and he became my mentor and trusted advisor. Joe was a chief technology officer at a fast-growing tech company in Austin. He was in his sixties and had been a hard-charging leader who got things done. He was small in stature, but his personality was big, and he commanded respect. He took me under his wing and taught me how to be a great salesperson. More importantly, he believed in me, and I deeply admired him; I still do. I spent years developing a solid relationship with him, and even though I had hidden this side of myself from him, I knew I could trust him to listen—and to help.

I broke down and told him everything: how I was addicted, broke, and filled with shame and self-hatred. He put his hand on my knee and said, "I will help you. But only if you help yourself. You must choose to live, or you will choose to die. You are responsible for where you are today. No one else. Unless you accept responsibility for your life and your choices, you'll never live up to your potential."

Ouch. But that's what a good mentor and friend does: keeps it real.

There was only one other person I could turn to—my mother. She knew I experimented with drugs, but I had never been totally honest with her. I didn't know how to be. If I were honest, it would mean admitting that I was lost, struggling, and not truly living a successful life. But I felt I had no other choice; I needed to go home. In fact, my heart was aching with homesickness. *Maybe I need to go home because that's where I belong*, I thought. *Maybe I won't be so lonely if I am close to my mom again . . .*

So, later that day, I swallowed my pride and called my mother to tell her everything. To my immense relief, she simply said, "Come home."

As reality sank in, my relief turned to fear, and I wondered, *What am I going to do when I get home?* After I left for college, my mother had moved to Durango, a small rural town in southwest Colorado. It's a beautiful place, but there aren't a lot of great jobs. And I was broke. But I knew I wanted to change my life, and the only way I was going to change it was by moving home and getting a job that would help me get out from under $100,000 of credit card debt.

The first step was to tell my boss I was leaving the company to go home. I couldn't tell him the truth about my addiction, so I made up a story about my dad being sick, which is ironic since I rarely spoke to my dad. The company was so kind to me, allowing me to stay on until I decided to move to Durango, even though I was underperforming and already knew I would be relocating. Looking back, I wonder if my boss believed my story. It had to be clear that I was in bad shape. But nonetheless, his compassion made the move easier, and I am grateful for his support.

Six weeks after my overdose, with most of my belongings in storage, I drove the thousand miles from Austin to Durango repeatedly crying, wondering what the hell I was doing. *How will I make it in Durango? Can I get a job?* And really, *I am twenty-eight and leaving my life in*

Austin to move back in with my mom? How humiliating. This is not success. There is nothing to be recognized for in this mess.

The only thoughts that relieved my anxiety were: *I have a place to live, and thank God for my mom.*

I had hit rock bottom. But I was also determined to take ownership of my life.

On the day of my interview, I was prepared and dressed to the nines. Of course, I went to the wrong door, and after knocking, the shipping clerk let me in. I'll never forget the look on her face when I told her I was there to interview for the general manager position. "Oh boy, I soooo hope they hire you!" she said with a half-smile, half-smirk on her face. Deanna still works for StoneAge, and we giggle every time we retell the story of how I got hired.

I met with John Wolgamott and Jerry Zink, cofounders of StoneAge, for a few hours. I answered their questions to the best of my ability, trying to balance confidence and humility. I did not want to repeat my earlier mistakes of overstating my experience and capabilities. The last thing I wanted to do was overpromise and underdeliver. Plus, there was no hiding the fact that I was underqualified. I walked out having no idea what they thought, feeling unsure that I would move to the next round.

When I got the call from StoneAge's HR manager to schedule an interview with the management team, I was relieved and excited. A few days later, I was back at StoneAge, knocking on the shipping door so Deanna would see that I had made it to round two, ready to meet my future team. After meeting with the seven managers, I felt confident they would pick me. They had expressed how scared they were that someone with a lot of experience would come in and change the culture. Obviously, they didn't like the candidates I was up against, and the mix of my inexperience, drive, and passion was somehow less intimidating.

But after my round-two interview, there were crickets. I waited. And waited. When I received a job offer from another company, I emailed the HR manager, telling her I had another offer, but I was hoping to hear from StoneAge one way or another so I could make my decision.

"John sent you an email," she replied.

"That's weird. I didn't get an email from John. Can you confirm what day he sent it?"

A few hours passed before she replied, "It looks like he actually sent the email to me, although it was addressed to you. I didn't look to verify that he included your email in the To field. I shouldn't have made that assumption, and I am so sorry. We would like to make you an offer; can you come by tomorrow to discuss it further?"

Wow, that was close. What if I hadn't followed up? Would they have written me off as a flake or unprofessional? Would they have reached back out? I'll never know the answer to these questions, but it was a powerful lesson. Always follow up, always understand the process, and never assume that silence is a no. Remember that even when it may seem like you're not in control, you can still take ownership of any circumstance you're in.

• • •

It wasn't long after I started working at StoneAge before I realized it was a very different kind of company than I'd ever worked at before. I know, I know, many leaders and founders say this about their company. But I genuinely believe that StoneAge is.

Started in a garage in 1979, when I was only one year old (as I often remind the founders), StoneAge has always been a company that cares. Cofounders John Wolgamott and Jerry Zink are the two most generous and brilliant people I know. They met at Colorado School of Mines while Jerry was a graduate student in the Mining department and John was a research assistant. Soon, the two came up with an idea to revolutionize the uranium mining industry: a rock drill that used water jets to safely and cleanly produce a hole for the placement of dynamite. After Jerry graduated, they both moved back to Jerry's hometown of Durango to start StoneAge, Inc.

Then the Three Mile Island accident happened, and everything changed.

On March 28, 1979, the most consequential nuclear accident in US history took place when a reactor at Three Mile Island Unit 2 Reactor near Middletown, Pennsylvania, had a partial meltdown. Spewing large amounts of nuclear reactor coolant, the failed reactor released radioactive gases and iodine into the environment. Luckily, epidemiological studies showed no increase in cancer rates in the area, but the cleanup spanned thirteen years and cost over $1 billion. The accident, highlighting the dangers of nuclear power generation, sparked anti-nuclear activism among the general public. The meltdown was the final nail in the coffin in an already declining industry; no new reactor construction meant a decrease in the need for uranium. This significantly impacted StoneAge, as its water jet rock drill's value proposition was to make uranium mining easier and safer.

Left with no customers but a strong belief in their product, they survived on civil engineering projects until they were invited to one of the first Waterjet Technology Association conferences held at Colorado School of Mines. There, John and Jerry met a group of men from a large industrial cleaning contractor out of Houston, Texas, who said, "If you can drill rock with that thing, let's see if you can drill plastic out of a heat exchanger." They proved that the tool could, in fact, be used for industrial cleaning applications, and that was how they pivoted from mining to industrial cleaning.

To give you a better idea of how StoneAge's tools work, imagine you are cleaning something with your garden hose. When you put your thumb over the hose end, you reduce the flow and create more pressure, making it easier to clean. Now imagine that water spinning. That's what we create, rotary nozzles that clean using high-pressure water. Water pressure starts at 2,500 psi and goes up to 40,000 psi. For context, the water pressure at a car wash is about 7,000 psi, enough to remove dirt but not paint. The kind of pressure we create with our tools can kill people. It's incredibly dangerous. We have also engineered some of our industry's most reliable automated cleaning equipment as we have evolved. Our equipment includes hose feed devices and positioning frames that remove the hose and nozzle from the hands of the waterblast operator, reducing injuries and making cleaning jobs more efficient. This equipment is now Internet of Things (IoT) enabled, which means it's smart and can collect and transmit data, giving our customers insight into how well they are cleaning.

I geek out on this stuff, which I still find slightly amusing. Never for the life of me would I have guessed I would be the CEO of a company that makes tools that clean sewers, tanks, and heat exchangers. But I love it, and I can't imagine being anywhere else.

While we invent useful and innovative products, this is not what makes us special. What makes us different is that we are employee owned.

In the late nineties, John and Jerry had a great idea to start selling stock to employees after a successful rollout of a robust profit-sharing plan. The idea was to generate capital without using bank debt while sharing in the success of the company's growth. Over a twenty-five-year period, employees bought 40 percent of the company, a remarkable feat and one that solidified our future as an employee-owned company. In 2015, we transitioned to an ESOP (Employee Stock Ownership Plan), allowing a more sustainable succession plan.

To help you understand StoneAge better, I want to share our Own It Mindset with you. It's important I take some time to share how ownership as a value and practice fits in to the company I serve each and every day. This is a pivotal component to my leadership, and I've seen this approach help countless others. The Own It Mindset is a set of behaviors that successful employees exhibit; it's our values and purpose for being. It has evolved, and this version is by far the most clearly articulated. After becoming an ESOP in 2015, we knew we needed to help our employees understand what it takes to be a successful employee–owner at StoneAge, as most people have no idea what this means and how it translates into what they do and how they show up. Plus, our ESOP would generate significant wealth for long-term employees, and I wanted to be sure that we attracted and retained the right employees and—quite frankly—helped those who didn't exhibit the Own It Mindset to move on.

Our Philosophy

Guided by the vision of our founders and the dedication of our employee–owners, StoneAge creates an impactful and positive presence in the lives of our employees, customers, and local communities. By staying true to our core values of creating rewarding jobs and constructive culture, engineering industry-leading products and services, and providing an exceptional customer experience, we will sustain and grow our company culture, customer loyalty, and long-term business success. Our mission is to inspire our employees and customers to say, "Why would I choose anyone but StoneAge?"

We use creativity, resolve, and comprehensive job performance to equip our customers with exceptional products, training, and expertise. We listen to our customers. We work diligently to solve their problems and adapt to market changes, drive business success, and enable safe work for their employees. We share our technical expertise freely to promote and facilitate safety, efficiency, and productivity across our industry.

We encourage our employees to view their careers at StoneAge as life-long opportunities for personal growth, professional accomplishment, and fulfillment. We provide a robust compensation and benefits package, support our employees' health and well-being, and create flexible schedules to help them fulfill family responsibilities and personal ambitions.

We are pleased to have a positive impact on our communities. We know that great jobs add to the vibrancy and health of the places we live. We believe in partnering with area charities and sourcing locally when possible. We model responsible stewardship of our facilities, environment, and natural resources.

The StoneAge Own It Mindset includes three fundamental values. These values allow us to deliver on promises to ourselves and our customers.

1. Be a great teammate.
2. Practice self-leadership.
3. Deliver on the StoneAge Assurance Promise.

Own It inspires us to incorporate the following with our values to sustain StoneAge as a leader in the industry:

- Use intellect to innovate, problem-solve, and learn continuously.
- Use empathy and curiosity to connect with each other.
- Use accountability to course-correct, make choices, and see the big picture.

Own It also inspires us to blend the following with our values:

- Preserve the business welfare and advancement of StoneAge while preserving individual, fundamental human needs to make a living.
- Work as a team to accomplish our promise to our customers and to appreciate the value of camaraderie.
- Bring intensity, passion, and excitement to our work and our customers.

Own It has specifics. The specifics can unfold differently for each individual, but there are some common elements:

Be a Great Teammate

At StoneAge, teamwork is fundamental to our success, and our actions define what it means to be a great teammate. Teamwork is a crucial value at StoneAge—it's part of our forty-year history and will catalyze and enable a successful future.

Great teammates show up every day willing to put their creativity, energy, honesty, and time toward the achievement and growth of themselves, their peers, teams, and the company overall. This perspective requires having an outward mindset and always assuming good intentions.

Great teammates are **humble, motivated**, and **relationship-builders**.

Humble: When we are humble, we accept we have strengths and non-strengths. We understand we have beneficial qualities and not-so-beneficial qualities. Great teammates are skillful teammates, and we activate strengths and beneficial qualities while restraining ways in which we can be wrongfully disruptive. Humble means we own mistakes, are accountable for our attitudes and aren't afraid to show vulnerability. Humble means we have our ego curbed. We are quick to point out the contributions of others; we share credit, emphasize team over self, and define success collectively rather than individually. Humble teammates are rewarded with recognition because their teammates appreciate their support, effort, and accountability.

Motivated: When we are motivated, we are stimulated and inspired; we want to influence in a resourceful way. Motivated teammates take stock of how they can encourage themselves and others within the capacity of their strengths and qualities. They are motivated to work on their personal purpose with purpose. They are proactive and thoughtful. If challenges or conflicts arise, they use skillful communication to confront what needs to be addressed.

Relationship-builder: Great teammates build strong relationships with their coworkers; they respect their teammates and support each other with advice and constructive feedback. They pay attention and adjust to team dynamics and understand the impact of their words and actions. They work across functions and teams to break down silos, share experiences, and help each other solve problems. A skillful teammate cares about others and would try to never undermine their team, peers, or the company with gossip. They know toxicity erodes relationships and undermines teamwork; they hold themselves and others accountable by calling out and ceasing toxic behaviors that damage our culture. Relationship-building teammates are rewarded with increased well-being because they contribute to strong relationships and healthy teams.

Practice Self-Leadership

Self-leadership does not unfold the same for everyone, but there are common threads. Self-leadership means you will be forthright to say you don't know. Self-leadership means owning your decisions and the associated successes or mistakes. Self-leadership means you are willing to work on your self-development as well as strengthen your skills and talents. Simply put: it's how you lead yourself. When you lead yourself well, your performance and attitude stand out, and you become a role model for others.

These are key aspects of self-leadership shared by StoneAge employee–owners:

- **Take care of yourself.** Nobody knows you better than you. Take responsibility for your health, fulfillment, and attitude. Have honest conversations with your manager about your overall well-being. Remember that self-care is a discipline, not a luxury.
- **Be self-aware.** Practice self-reflection to assess how you contributed to a situation and commit to responding with your best self. Understand how you affect your peers and the teams' shared outcomes. Your attitude and effort matter.
- **Be responsible for understanding.** Every person should know how they support the company's mission and culture, so take responsibility for understanding how you contribute. Be curious and ask questions; this perspective fuels inclusivity, proactivity, and creativity.
- **Be resilient.** Bounce back from setbacks with resolve and persistence. Have the viewpoint that challenging problems are tasks to be mastered. Believe that you can handle anything that comes your way.
- **Take the initiative.** Don't wait to be told what to do or expect other people to solve problems for you. Raise your hand and volunteer. Make suggestions for improvement. Never settle for mediocrity.
- **Be accountable.** Own your attitude, effort, and mistakes. Avoid complaining and blaming; instead, ask yourself: *What can I do to make things better?*

- **Keep it real**. Provide direct, timely, and caring feedback—always to help others be their best. Ask others to return the favor and commit to gracefully receiving feedback.
- **Be brave**. Our employees are what makes StoneAge special. Share your ideas, support each other, and ask for help when you need it. Be okay with failing; we are learning every day, and we grow and improve by making mistakes.

Deliver on the StoneAge Assurance Promise

And finally, work we do to become great teammates and excel at self-leadership is for naught if we didn't take care of our customers. That's why we all live and breathe the StoneAge Assurance Promise: StoneAge does what it takes to help our customers complete their jobs easily, safely, on time, and on budget.

The expectations and commitments we all make to owning our role—whether it is as an executive, manager, or individual contributor—allow us to realize sustained success. This approach to nurturing a successful company shows every employee that their contributions matter and have an impact on the growth we all benefit from.

What Is Employee Ownership Anyway, and Why Does It Matter?

Like many CEOs and business leaders, I've given a lot of thought to income inequality and the shrinking middle class. While this far-reaching societal issue is complex and can't be solved overnight, leaders can make a real difference in their employees' lives through more equitable compensation and benefits.

While generous compensation can make a significant difference in the day-to-day lives of our teams, salaries alone aren't enough to help employees build real savings and wealth. In our economy, the costs of living are very high relative to the average person's pay, especially considering the current inflationary issues we face. Many people are living paycheck to paycheck, which is a risky and fragile situation. We used to think that going to college was the best path to a better, more wealthy life, but skyrocketing tuition and crushing debt makes it inaccessible for many. Now, even higher degrees do not guarantee a higher salary.

Employee ownership is a broad term; it infers that a company's employees own stock in the company. There are many different forms of employee ownership, ranging from stock grants to more complex plans like an employee stock ownership plan (ESOP). Founders or business leaders have many reasons why they believe employee ownership is a viable model for their companies. For example, employee ownership can assist with founder succession, increasing the company's performance, building a robust retirement plan for employees, and creating a strong culture where employees have a voice and share in company success.

An ESOP is essentially an ownership model that is best accessed at retirement, similar to a 401(k) plan, but instead of investing in the stock market, the ESOP trust buys company stock and holds its assets in a trust for employees. An ESOP can own just a small percentage of the company or up to 100 percent of it. ESOP participants—the company's employees—accrue shares in the plan over time and are paid out by having their shares repurchased, typically after leaving the company. If they are of retirement age, they can take the payout as cash. If they are not of retirement age, they can roll it into a private individual retirement account (IRA).

There are other types of equity compensation models, but I won't go into them in detail here. If you would like more information on them, you can visit the National Center for Employee Ownership (NCEO) website (www.nceo.org).

Philip Kotler, a professor at the Kellogg School of Management at Northwestern University, wrote an article in 2021 on worker discontent that makes a good case for employee ownership.* He wrote,

> *Deeper understanding of the worker discontent problem can come from looking at the structure of management/labor relations. Companies exist to create value; value is created with Capital and Labor; Capital gets to keep the profits (or losses); ordinary Labor only gets a salary and has no other means of support; yet Labor might be responsible for creating between 40–70 percent of the profit. Marxian economists hold that labor creates most of the value, but most of the profits go to Capital (shareholders). Workers are never able to earn enough to buy shares in their or other companies to become capitalists. Under these conditions, workers become alienated and will just do enough work to get by and not be fired. There is little they will gain by working harder. They are without any ownership or any voice in where their company is or should be going.*

This statement sums up why I am such a believer in employee ownership. I have seen firsthand the benefits in sharing the success of the company. Ownership opportunities, if done right, can create a culture of engagement and purpose. Employees feel that they have growth opportunities. If they work hard and add value for the company's customers, they will directly benefit, not only by feeling valued and included but also by increased bottom lines.

According to the NCEO, 6,500 companies now offer ESOPs in

---

* Philip Kotler, "Should Workers Own Stock in Their Companies?" Medium, February 20, 2021, https://4pkotler.medium.com/should-workers-own-stock-in-their-companies-47b8e837405e.

which 14 million Americans participate; another 9 million companies have given employees stock options.* Even Harley-Davidson has embraced employee ownership. It has issued stock to 4,500 of its employees, including all its hourly factory workers.†

Setting up an employee-ownership program can be complicated, and companies may get discouraged if they attempt it independently. There is no coordination around employee ownership in the federal government and no agency to guide them. We began our journey by attending an NCEO workshop for companies considering ESOPs, which was incredibly helpful. From there we found attorneys, accountants, and advisors specializing in employee ownership. If you are considering employee ownership, I highly recommend perusing the NCEO website and getting in touch with an attorney who specializes in ESOPs. Many inexperienced advisors will give you incorrect advice or even discourage you from pursuing employee ownership, which is unfortunate, as it's such an empowering ownership transition model.

In Colorado, Governor Jared Polis made employee ownership a priority in his administration partially to address income inequality and partly to battle the "silver tsunami"—the impact of Baby Boomer business owners retiring and wanting to exit their companies. The Colorado Employee Ownership Commission he set up has made it easier for local companies to learn about employee ownership. The Colorado Employee Ownership Office provides technical assistance. Many states could jump-start their progress by setting up a similar office. I feel fortunate to sit on this commission, educating business

---

* "What Is Employee Ownership?" National Center for Employee Ownership, accessed October 2022, https://www.nceo.org/what-is-employee-ownership#_Toc529288092.

† Chibuike Oguh, "Harley Davidson adopts KKR executive-inspired employee stock program," Reuters, February 2, 2021, https://www.reuters.com/article/us-harley-davidson-workers-idUSKBN2A22SI.

leaders on its benefits and advocating for tax incentives to offset the high set-up costs.

I believe that employee ownership could help preserve local economies and middle-class jobs as the "silver tsunami" sweeps through the nation. With many older owners getting ready to retire, job-creating businesses in many communities are likely to close or get gobbled up by private equity firms. Embracing employee ownership could offer current owners a way to cash out that protects jobs in their communities and allows teams that truly care about keeping the business intact to stay on. It's ultimately a way to build a stronger financial future—for the company, the community, and workers who might not otherwise have a chance to build wealth for themselves and their families.

How to Lead an Employee-Owned Company

I am often asked, "How do you get anything done if everyone is an owner and you have to vote on all decisions?"

That's not how employee ownership works. Management is responsible for running the company. Only a few decisions are voted on by employee shareholders, such as dissolving the company or selling to an acquiring company. As CEO of an ESOP company, I am ultimately responsible for ensuring that we grow profitability and responsibly.

But I also lead differently than other CEOs. Unlike many CEOs who share limited financial information in fear of how it might be used by their employees, StoneAge is an open-book company and shares real-time financial performance with all employees. Rather than keep people in the dark, I am incredibly transparent and communicate regularly about our leadership teams' decisions, including explaining why we are making them. Instead of making top-down decisions, we ask for input and ideas, seek feedback from all levels of the organization, and try to give as much authority and autonomy as possible to everyone in the organization. I believe that if you treat people like adults, they will act like adults. In fact, I so deeply believe this way that I don't bother with non-compete agreements. I might get burned once or twice, but the goodwill and belief in people's inherent good helps them believe it in themselves.

Is it always pretty? No. Is it easy? Rarely. Do we make mistakes in how and when we communicate? Absolutely. And we wouldn't have it any other way. Our culture is made up of the collective. Yes, it's leadership's responsibility to set the tone, address issues, and lead by example. But each person either adds to or takes away from our culture, and we expect our employees to exhibit the Own It Mindset. Doing so not only creates a dynamic and fun workplace, but it also pays. Successful employees in a successful ESOP company are well rewarded. This is how you build a culture of ownership. And this is how you build the middle class from the middle out.

PART TWO
LEADING YOURSELF

3

FIND YOUR PURPOSE

What is your personal purpose? How do you find purpose in what you do so that you can make a lasting impact? It comes from a combination of things: being of service to others, trying new things, stretching yourself around your strengths and weaknesses, and being good at what you do. In my opinion, this is how you bring value to the world. And it's also how you take ownership in leading yourself.

Aligning your work with personal purpose is an integral part of being fulfilled at work. In fact, it's often advised to "do what you love; turn your passion into your work!" Despite its feel-good intent, this is not great counsel. "Passion is not something you follow," says Cal Newport, author of *So Good They Can't Ignore You: Why Skills Trump Passion in the Search for Work You Love.* "Passion is something that will follow you as you put in the hard work to become valuable to the world."

When I was ten years old, I knew I wanted the freedom that making my own money gave me. I also knew that I didn't want to be poor.

My mother was always able to make ends meet but barely. We weren't poor, but we didn't have much. My mom sometimes worked three jobs to make sure we had a roof over our heads, food on the table, and a little extra to do something fun every summer. She didn't say it, but I knew she always worried about money. Even though I was young, I could tell she wasn't motivated by making money. Her intrinsic motivation was helping others, even if it meant she had nothing left over for herself. And I love her dearly for this life view.

She moved to Montrose, Colorado, when my grandfather gave up a successful career in corporate retail to go out on his own. His lifelong dream was to live out West. My grandfather grew up dirt poor—the floor of his house was literally dirt. But he managed to put himself through college using the GI bill and earned a business degree. He spent his career in retail, working his way up the ladder at JC Penney and then the May Company, where he became a vice president. But he hated his corporate role at the May Company. The culture was awful, and he went home every day feeling unfulfilled, frustrated, and disappointed.

But my grandfather was a true leader and brilliant businessman. In the 1960s, he taught himself stock market investing, and soon, he had made enough to buy a sporting goods retail business in rural Colorado. He quit his job at the May Company in 1971 after only five years as a VP, taking a considerable risk, as he was the sole breadwinner for his wife and six children.

My mother, who was eighteen years old at the time, left Washington, DC, to help him get started. She worked endless hours helping him get his store off the ground. Seven years later, she had me, and she knew retail was not her passion. She left my grandfather's business and worked on an assembly line at a manufacturing company and the night shift at a local motel, among other things. But the job she loved the most was working as a classroom assistant.

When I was twelve years old, she decided to go to college to get a bachelor's degree to become a teacher. She drove eighty miles each way, three days a week, from our home south of Montrose, Colorado, to Gunnison, Colorado, to get her degree. Anyone who has driven that stretch of road knows that it can be treacherous, especially in the winter. She graduated with summa honors while working full time. It was inspiring to watch as a young woman. It was also motivating. While I was proud of my mother and loved her dearly, I knew I wanted something more. I wanted to make more money to feel more secure and in control of my future. Although I wasn't sure at the time exactly how I'd earn a living, I knew I needed to start working early.

My first job was babysitting. I never enjoyed doing that work, but it was a great way to learn how to be responsible for another living being. I began umpiring and scorekeeping softball when I was ten, and when I was twelve, I talked my grandfather into letting me work in his store. I started helping customers find what they were looking for, and soon, I ran the cash register. I worked after school and on weekends, and when my aunt, who oversaw buying, asked me my thoughts on what kind of merchandise she should buy, I was thrilled. I loved flipping through the catalogs and marking styles I thought would be big sellers. I felt a sense of pride when some of the styles I picked flew off the shelves and was curious when others didn't. I asked customers about their choices and what they didn't like about certain styles and products. I innately understood that to be successful in business, you had to understand your customers and work hard to give them what they want. In this case, it was a good shopping experience. My favorite times were when celebrities came into the store. Montrose is a feeder town to Telluride, one of the most magical ski towns on the planet, and even from its earliest days it attracted the rich and famous. I took note of everything celebrities bought so I could advise my aunt on what to buy next.

By the time I was fifteen years old, I managed inventory for my grandfather's three store locations, including receiving, price marking, and ensuring the correct product went to the right location. I loved running the "marking room." It was in the basement of an ancient brick building with an old-fashioned pull-chain-operated freight elevator. I could listen to the music of my choice, create my schedule, and most importantly, add real value to the family operation. I loved this job. It taught me to enjoy work, especially when I was doing something I was good at and felt like I had an important role.

Although I took on a lot of responsibility as a teen and loved building my work ethic, I was still young, and I had a lot more to learn. In my sophomore year in high school, I was a mess. I dated an older guy who was trouble. I skipped school and drank too much. After a fight with my mom, I moved out of my house and in with a friend. I was only sixteen years old, but I thought I knew how to run my life better than anyone else.

Three days after I had moved out, my mom called me and told me to come home immediately. She had just returned from my high school principal's office after being called in to look at signatures on the many excused absence notes I had turned in after missing many classes. So that I wouldn't get expelled, she only picked out a dozen or so of the many, many forged letters.

"What the hell are you doing with your life?" she asked me after confronting me about the forged signatures. "I don't care what you do after you graduate, but when you are eighteen, you are out of this house. I don't care if you work at Walmart for the rest of your life. You are not living here one more day after graduation. And that's *if* you even graduate!"

I was stunned. Did she think I was a failure? Not smart enough to go to college? Not worthy enough?

"You don't think I'm going to college, Mom?" I asked defiantly.

"Why would I think that?" she replied. "You don't go to school now. The path you are on is not going to lead to college. You have so much potential, but you are blowing it for a loser boyfriend and the next party. Unless you make some changes, you're going to be stuck here for the rest of your life!"

What a wake-up call. I knew that my mom truly did care about what I did with my life, and she didn't want me to work at Walmart, but her frustrations with my behavior were overwhelming for her. And her anger struck a chord within me. There was no doubt in my mind that I was going to go to college, but at that moment, I clearly saw that my behaviors and actions were not in alignment with the goal of leaving my hometown to create a different kind of life for myself. I saw that others perceived me as a troublemaker, a person who wasn't living up to her potential—maybe they even saw me as a loser. I wanted people to see me as intelligent, talented, and successful.

At that moment, I knew I needed to buckle down and do the work.

I was always good at math and curious about science. Throughout high school, my teachers encouraged me to study engineering. I didn't fully understand what engineers did, but I learned engineers were some of the highest-paid professionals right out of college. That was enough motivation for me. A small, academically rigorous engineering and science college in Golden, Colorado—Colorado School of Mines (aka Mines)—seemed like my best bet. It wasn't easy to get into, but I knew people would see me as smart and talented if accepted. Mines also had a softball team, which was a sport I loved and played as a varsity athlete. This fateful conversation with my mother was the catalyst for my decision to settle down and do the work required to get accepted to Mines and win a softball scholarship.

Yes, I was only sixteen, but I quit drinking that day and asked a team-mate's parent to film me at practice and in games. After I put together my recruitment film, I sent it to the softball coach at Mines and convinced her to come to watch me play at the state softball tournament. After watching several games throughout my junior and senior years, the coach told me if I were to be accepted into the School of Mines, she would grant me a full-tuition scholarship. I studied hard for my ACTs, maintained straight-A grades, and kept out of trouble.

Mines was the only college I applied to. I was confident I would be accepted, and I wasn't interested in going anywhere else. When I told my absentee dad my plan, he replied, "Are you sure that's where you want to go? Are you smart enough to graduate from engineering school? Maybe you should apply to journalism school instead."

Interestingly, my love of writing has come full circle, and one of my fondest memories of high school was being the copy editor and editor-in-chief of our school's newspaper. I even won several awards for journalistic writing. But what I heard from my dad was, "You're not smart enough." Without pausing to consider that my dad might have a point, I became even more determined to make Mines happen.

The hard work paid off, and when I received the acceptance letter, along with a letter of intent from the Mines softball coach, I breathed a sigh of relief. I had done it.

During the first semester of my sophomore year at Mines, I realized that I did not want to be an engineer. While being good at math is a prerequisite for engineering, it does not guarantee that you will actually be a sound engineer. I had zero interest in design, and the only classes I enjoyed were my math and humanities classes. In fact, my favorite class in all four years I was there was Introduction to Religion, where I experienced the plethora of spiritual practices and belief systems throughout the world for the first time. Clearly, I am not meant to be an engineer, and you wouldn't want to use anything I designed in my classes out of fear for your safety.

But there was no way I was quitting. I had to prove that I could graduate from Mines. Plus, I loved my softball team, and my scholarship paid for tuition. My mother couldn't afford to send me to college without a scholarship. So, I stuck it out, finding that I enjoyed taking business classes and could imagine myself in management someday. I put my head down, took summer school, worked my butt off, and graduated in four years. I have few friends from Mines, and those memories are weak and fleeting. Graduation day is the only thing I really remember from those four years.

These experiences were probably the most important aspect of my youth. Working hard is what I do. I am lucky that I was able to learn this at a young age, and I am forever grateful to my grandfather and my Aunt Mary for giving me to the opportunity to gain this kind of experience. The thread carries through all that I do and is what pulled me through my darkest moments.

Most highly skilled people become that way because they worked hard to become their best. Take Michael Jordan, for example, who is widely considered to be the best basketball player of all time. Remarkably, he was not a standout basketball player in his adolescence. Considered too short by his coaches, he didn't make his sophomore basketball team. Embarrassed by the failure, he channeled this rejection into motivation to practice more and better than anyone else. He was first at the gym and last to leave; he believed he would get out of the game what he put into it. And because he worked to be good at basketball, it became his passion. Once it became his passion, he overcame all obstacles. And once he realized it took a team, he became a legend when he started serving the team rather than himself.

While most of us will never be the Michael Jordan of our professions, we can learn from his dedication to hard work, practicing, building upon his strengths, making weaknesses strengths, and ultimately serving his team and fans. It's rewarding to be great at something, and since you spend eight-plus hours a day at work, you must find purpose in your work. If you do, it might just turn into your passion.

Purpose isn't something that suddenly appears—at least not for most; it's something that evolves. It's deeply personal and can't be handed to you. I found mine through learning what I didn't want to do, almost killing myself, taking a few risks, joining a company where the culture was a good fit, and working my ass off to improve continuously.

Looking back through years of journaling, one thread has always been there: my purpose to be an impactful leader who helps people create more meaningful lives for themselves. It's really that simple, but I didn't always know this was my purpose. In fact, I believe that being purposeless, combined with feeling lonely, led me to addiction. It took me doing many things I didn't like, such as going engineering school, working in sales, moving away from my roots, and numbing my feelings of inadequacy to finally find my purpose of being a high-impact, disruptive leader. It took me finding the right role within the right company before it appeared so clearly. And I certainly have questioned my purpose along the way, losing focus from time to time but always coming back to it. Impacting other people's lives is what I love to do, whether I'm parenting, running a company, advising, writing, podcasting, or speaking.

As I've matured, I've realized that I can make such an impact through my words and effort, so I practice constantly defining and refining my message; listening deeply; and then speaking, writing, and asking questions with *clear purpose and intention*. Why do I emphasize *with clear purpose and intention*? Because this is how I become of service to others. I shape my thoughts and words to provide the most value possible to those who read and listen. The more I practice, the more I improve. The more I improve, the wider my audience becomes—and the more I am living my purpose.

Another aspect of my purpose is to push myself to do hard things to see what I can accomplish, physically, mentally, and spiritually. When I read Viktor Frankl's *Man's Search for Meaning*, his philosophy that we find purpose in suffering resonated. He said, "In some ways, suffering ceases to be suffering at the moment it finds meaning." Frankl's statement resonated with me because I find purpose in my own suffering. I truly know that my suffering has meaning. There is pain and hardship in pursuing impact, in pushing yourself beyond what you thought possible, and in ignoring people who tear you down or work against you. But making an impact is meaningful, and the suffering further engrains my purpose—making it more real and meaningful.

Put It into Practice: How to Find Your Purpose

Try new things.

I am grateful for my previous crappy jobs and ineffective bosses because they taught me much about what I *didn't* want. These negative experiences are more powerful than the positive ones in shaping my purpose. I watched the leaders in those companies and analyzed their effort, styles, and how they ran their organizations. I volunteered, sat on a school board, chaired the local economic development organization, spoke at events, and wrote articles. I tried an engineering job, a sales job, and an operations management job. I ran a few ultramarathons, got into and quit CrossFit, and hated mountain biking for years before I fell in love with the sport. All these experiences helped me shape my purpose. Don't be afraid to try new things to expand your experiences, skills, and competencies.

Take some risks.

Packing up my life and moving to Durango with no money and no job was risky—even though it was riskier for my well-being and health to stay in Texas. Applying for a job I was grossly underqualified for was gutsy but worth the chance of rejection. Getting on stage in front of thousands of people and sharing my deeply personal stories takes courage. Saying no to opportunities that distracted me felt bold. To find your purpose, you must take risks, pushing boundaries of what you thought possible and expanding your competency zone. It feels good to do hard things—doing them will help you find your purpose.

Build a community.

Finding passion and feeling purposeful is hard if you don't belong. There is power in being part of a community, people who believe in you, support you, and push you to become better. I found my purpose through my mother's support as well as that of my teammates and employees, the founders of StoneAge, my board, and my community of readers and listeners. Their encouragement and belief in me pushed me to keep going, expand my capabilities, and put myself out there. Surround yourself with people like this. Build a culture that is supportive, inclusive, and encourages both personal and professional growth. As Brené Brown says, "Connection gives purpose and meaning to our lives."

Give your best effort.

There is a saying, "Mastery leads to purpose," which I wholeheartedly believe. The more I write, the better I become. The better I become, the more I enjoy doing it and the more impactful messages I create. Making an impact is my purpose. See how it works? Channel Michael

Jordan: practice, practice, and more practice. Look at new tasks and challenges as strength and conditioning exercises; with every task complete and challenge overcome, you've built your "getting good at your job" muscles. Give your best effort and analyze your performance. Then practice more. Mastery will lead to purpose over time.

Never stop learning.

Working with a writing coach and speaking coach expands my knowledge, opens doors, and helps refine my skills. Working with my brilliant board of directors, asking questions, and gleaning insight from their experiences makes me a better CEO. Reading leadership and business books gives me new ideas and shapes my thinking on leadership, culture, and business growth. Honing your craft, expanding your knowledge, and meeting people who teach you things along the way expands your worldview, piques your curiosity, and allows you to examine and shape your purpose.

Don't be afraid to change.

As I've said, purpose evolves and may even change as you mature and grow. That's okay. Your purpose and passions will change as you change; let them evolve and let go of what no longer feels meaningful and true. Like all things in life, there is no final destination for your purpose in life. Get comfortable with the ebb and flow and embrace feelings of confusion when you are transitioning to a new stage in life. It's all part of the journey.

• • •

I'll leave you with one of my favorite Viktor Frankl quotes:

> *It did not really matter what we expected from life but rather what life expected from us. We needed to stop asking about the meaning of life and think of ourselves as those who were being questioned by life—daily and hourly. Our answer must consist not in talk and meditation but in right action and right conduct. Life ultimately means taking the responsibility to find the right answer to its problems and to fulfill the tasks which it constantly sets for each individual.*

4

ASK POWERFUL QUESTIONS

I am often asked how you learn to be a CEO. My answer is simple: the only way to learn is by *being* a CEO. And I started learning how to be a CEO by asking questions. A lot of questions. A common mistake many leaders make is assuming they must appear to know all the answers all the time, but this couldn't be further from the truth. Great leaders understand and welcome circumstances when they don't know exactly what to say or do. Great leaders aren't distracted by always being right; great leaders know how to ask the right questions to help them make the best decisions.

I had no idea what I was doing as I started my job at StoneAge back in 2007, so I did the only thing I could think of: I asked questions. My team was filled with knowledgeable, experienced people who had been with the company for some time. I figured they knew what was going well and what needed to be fixed.

There were many opportunities for me to ask questions that would lead me to making thoughtful decisions for the company. For example, early on there was frustration on the management team, as some people weren't pulling their weight, so we restructured the management team to be more effective. I started by asking the team what was working and what wasn't. I also asked them how they wanted to see the management team structured. They had excellent feedback, and it helped me better understand the team's dynamics. I implemented many of their suggestions. Additionally, the management team didn't work from budgets, so we developed a budgeting framework. I probed the team about how they made decisions and asked them how I could help them be more comfortable creating a budget. We implemented a budgeting process, and we grew by 22 percent that year. Our success that first year was built on ideas that weren't mine.

Every time I asked, "Why are we doing it this way, and do you have ideas on how to make it better?" I was given clear, actionable responses that I helped the team implement. My commitment to asking questions of others allowed me to be a better leader and facilitate growth and improvement.

I learned so much from this experience. Rather than come in and try to prove that I was worthy of the job by demanding change and doing it "my way," I coached my team on making the changes with me, and I involved them in the process by tapping them for their unique perspectives and experiences. I saw myself as a piece of the puzzle, and asking questions allowed me to find my fit within the culture rather than forcing the culture to change around me. I also gained powerful insight—insight that helped me understand myself and my team better. I developed stronger relationships in a short amount of time, and I built trust quickly. I believe I made better decisions by keeping an open mind and not being afraid to say, "I'm not sure what to do. What do you think?"

For decades, research has shown that people communicate for two primary reasons: 1) to enhance information or learn from one another, and 2) to build relationships and get to know others. Asking good questions achieves both, which is powerful. Several Harvard University professors collaborated to analyze conversations among participants who were casually learning about each other via speed dating or online chats.* Participants were told to ask many questions—at least nine in fifteen minutes—and others to ask very few questions—less than four in fifteen minutes. In both the online chat group and the speed-dating groups, the people who asked questions were better liked, and speed-dating participants were more willing to go on a second date with partners who asked more questions.

If you want to be a better leader, ask more questions. You will create deeper connections, gather more information that will help you make better decisions, and people will like you more. In fact, according to Gallup, the most successful companies have managers who think like coaches, not bosses.† It's a powerful experience when you have meaningful and purposeful conversations with people on your team. It helps to clarify goals and expectations, gives a framework to talk about performance and goals, and builds deeper relationships.

Put It into Practice:
How to Ask Powerful Questions

The best managers ask questions like:

- What would you like the outcome of this project to be?
- If you were me, what would you do to solve this problem?

---

* Alison Wood Brooks and Leslie K. John, "The Surprising Power of Questions," *Harvard Business Review*, May 2018, https://hbr.org/2018/05/the-surprising-power-of-questions.

† Jennifer Robison, "Turn Your Company into a Human Development Machine," Gallup, November 25, 2020, https://www.gallup.com/workplace/326339/turn-company-human-development-machine.aspx.

- What do you think?
- What role would you like to play in this project?
- What can you do to move this project along faster?
- How can I help?

Questions like these engage your team and allow them to be part of developing solutions. Asking for your employees' opinions makes them feel included and valued, which will help you achieve more because you grant people the power to solve their own problems and give input on their work. Plus, it's easier and more fun when you don't have to be the one who solves all the issues.

Knowing how to ask good questions is one of the most powerful tools you can have in your toolbox. Sadly, most of us are terrible at asking questions, and we don't even know it. We ask easy questions when we should be asking hard ones. We keep it superficial when we should be going deeper. We stop asking questions too soon—just when the answers are about to get interesting. We get tongue-tied, chicken out, make up excuses, give up, and don't ask.

Asking good questions will improve your life, relationships, career, and business. They allow you to get the most out of every interaction. More questions equal more insight, information, and knowledge. Who doesn't want more of that?

Want to improve your question-asking skills? Here are some of my tips.

Be genuinely curious.

I am often asked how I get people to open up to me quickly, and my response is simple: I am genuinely interested in what people say. My goal is to walk away from all my conversations having learned something more about the person, topic, or situation. To do that, I must ask meaningful questions that lead the discussion down the path to greater insight, connection, and knowledge. Being curious also inspires you to ask follow-up questions. According to Alison Wood Brooks, O'Brien Associate Professor of Business Administration at Harvard Business School, follow-up questions are the best way to get to the heart of any situation.* When you ask follow-up questions, you show the person you are talking with that you are listening, caring, and curious, making them feel respected and heard. The benefit to you is that you get more insight and information, which is helpful as a leader. The good thing about follow-up questions is that they come naturally; just keep asking.

Ask open-ended questions.

Asking yes-or-no questions is the fastest way to a dead-end conversation. The good news is that it's easy to tell when you've asked one: you will get a yes or a no. It seems rudimentary but asking who, what, when, where, why, and how questions will always give you better answers and will help you know what to ask next. If you are at a loss, say something like, "Tell me more about that."

Listen with both ears.

Don't let yourself be distracted by emails, texts, your thoughts, and your desire to tell your own story. When you listen with both ears, you are more likely to catch the nuances in the words, tone, and voice inflection, which, when explored, lead to deeper understanding. When you hear nuance or something that sparks your curiosity, ask a question as simple as, "What did you mean by that?" You'll gain more insight

---

* Alison Wood Brooks and Leslie K. John, "The Surprising Power of Questions," *Harvard Business Review*, May-June 2018, https://hbr.org/2018/05/the-surprising-power-of-questions.

if you are genuinely listening rather than planning your response or talking yourself.

Don't be afraid.

People are often too embarrassed to ask questions in fear of showing ignorance or being considered "too direct." Or perhaps they worry that asking probing questions will come across as intrusive or nosey, but I have found that most of the time, people want to open up, give answers, and share their stories. In my opinion, the worst kind of question is the one left unasked.

Practice, practice, practice.

Just like any skill, repetition will make you better. Before you go into a conversation, write down at least five open-ended questions you could ask. If you don't understand something, ask for more information, and don't stop until you feel like you've got it. If the person gives a benign answer, ask a question that takes him or her deeper. When you think the conversation is over, ask one more clarifying question. Don't be afraid to interject and ask a question in the middle of someone's story. Most people don't mind the interruption, and it shows that you are truly engaged. Your questioning skills will get better the more you ask, so practice, practice, practice.

Don't assume.

Believing that you know what the person's answer is will lead to miscommunications and false assumptions. Even if you think you know, ask anyway. Don't let the opportunity for further clarification and deeper understanding pass you by—you will be surprised at what you learn about the answer—and your assumptions.

• • •

I have found asking good questions has made me a better leader and person. They allow me to get past superficial answers and surface-level relationships and truly connect with those around me. These deeper connections have enriched my life and world. I have built the strongest of relationships through being curious about others. I have met amazing people in unassuming places because I am not afraid to make a personal inquiry. I have been able to help people in times of need and pain because I can ask questions that help them get to the root of the problem. I have increased self-awareness because I am not fearful of asking for feedback that gives me a deeper insight into myself and my effect on those around me. And I have gained valuable knowledge about my world that helps me make better business and life decisions.

"Ask, and thou shalt receive." I couldn't agree more.

5

ADOPT STRATEGIC LEADERSHIP

The world has always needed strong leaders, and we have witnessed how profound both exceptional and poor leadership can be. Today, the world faces unprecedented challenges: climate change, pandemics, government failure, and deep social and political polarization. Business leaders have the opportunity to impact these issues, not only through the creation of their products and services but through the way they lead and the cultures they create.

Every leader brings unique approaches to managing. No two leaders will think precisely the same when confronted with the same problem. Diverse, creative thinking is an incredible asset in any organization. Having leaders with varied approaches and styles makes developing and sustaining a holistic business approach more enjoyable and more successful. However, when each leader doesn't work to balance their strengths individually, companies may suffer as a result.

Great leaders can articulate a vision and a path to achieve that vision.

They can peer around the corner and anticipate what's coming. Great leaders know how to tie employee experience to customer experience, motivating the team to achieve success through the desire to improve their own lives and their customers' lives. Great leaders understand that employees who think and act like owners will create a culture that leads to profound success and impact.

Just because you have a leadership title doesn't mean you are leading *well*. To lead well, you must inspire, motivate, and build a team that shares a sense of purpose and ownership. To lead well, you need self-awareness, which allows you to see how your actions, words, and behaviors affect others, and you need to be honest with yourself when your teams need more or better from you. It is often in times of volatility that we learn how to deliver more as leaders, especially when there are livelihoods at stake.

My first year as a CEO was challenging. It was 2009, and sales were down from the previous year for the first time in StoneAge's history. The financial crisis had hit us, too, and I was stressed. I wasn't sure what to do. Questions of layoffs, pay cuts, even survival were running through my head. Every day I had moments in my office where I pondered *How will we get through this?*

As the financial crisis unfolded, I realized that this would be a defining moment in my leadership journey. When we look back on our lives, we never say, "That was so easy! I learned a lot from that experience!" It's usually the hard decisions and tough times that define our leadership. How we handle adversity is an important factor in determining leadership success. The decisions I made, how I made them, and how I communicated with my team set the stage for leading as a CEO. Strong leadership was needed, and I was determined to show that I was the right person for the job.

As I stood in front of my employees to tell them how we planned to handle falling sales revenue, I felt many emotions. Fearful yet hopeful, unsure but determined. I delivered the message that we were in this together, and we would all tighten our belts: There would be no raises and perhaps no profit sharing, but we wouldn't layoff anyone. We would cut all discretionary spending but continue to invest in R&D and international expansion.

The company pulled through the crisis stronger than ever. The team rallied and set record growth the following year, and I attribute this to stronger leadership throughout the organization. The leadership team told the truth and nothing but the truth. Transparency matters, and we shared the good, bad, and ugly. That being said, we set a clear vision and inspired our team to work hard to overcome setbacks brought on by the financial crisis. In *Leading at a Higher Level*, Ken Blanchard shares, "Leadership is about going somewhere. If you and your people don't know where you are going, your leadership doesn't matter."

Even though everyone forwent a raise, they knew we cared for them. We exhibited this with the compassionate and straightforward approach we took. I talked with every employee, asking their thoughts on the crisis and how we were handling it. We celebrated wins and recognized outstanding teamwork. We emphasized teamwork, and everyone knew we were in it together.

Every person desires a leader whom they trust, who gives them hope and provides compassion and stability. This isn't always easy in volatile times, but we created an even stronger culture by addressing employee issues head-on and talking through their concerns.

Truth be told, I got lucky. Yes, we made good decisions and it was the right move to focus on R&D and international expansion, but we did it without a well-thought-out plan. We executed well because we focused on our core business. We were good at delivering great products and great service, and we simply continued to do what we had been doing for the previous decade. Looking back, I realize that I used motivation and inspiration to keep us all focused and optimistic about the company rather than a well-thought-out strategy and tight management of the company. We did what we had to do, and luckily, we got it done. I took these lessons into 2020 when I was once again forced to make tough decisions and cuts. We were much more intentional about how we combined inspiration, transparency, strategy, and tightly executed management of the company to catapult us through the pandemic and position us to disrupt our industry.

The beginning of my journey as a CEO was not easy, and my leadership approach expanded immensely in my first years. Becoming a well-rounded leader takes both time and intention, and the first step is becoming aware of the type of leadership style you practice and how to grow other aspects of leadership styles into your approach. According to Glenn Rowe in his *Academy of Management Executive* article "Creating Wealth in Organizations: The Role of Strategic Leadership," there are three types of leaders: visionary, managerial, and strategic.

Visionary Leaders

Visionary leaders inspire by creating excitement about future possibilities. They are master storytellers and love ideas. Inspired to create, these leaders seek to shape the future and disrupt their industries. The downside is that most visionary leaders are bored by the day-to-day operations of a company. They are so focused on the future that they can lose sight of operational details, which can cause a company to crash and burn if left unchecked.

Managerial Leaders

Managerial leaders are lovers of budgets, processes, and policies and are inspired by managing an organization's day-to-day operations. Building in-depth knowledge about their businesses, they focus on operational efficiency and financial performance rather than rallying the organization around an inspirational vision of the future. While managerial leaders are critical to a well-run company, they risk creating a transactional culture that cares more about maintaining the status quo than investing in innovation and creativity, making the company less competitive over time.

Strategic Leaders

Strategic leaders can combine the other two types of leadership styles effectively. With an eye to the future, they can excite the organization about the direction of the company while at the same time ensuring that the company is well managed and meeting key performance indicators (KPIs) and financial performance requirements. Strategic leaders are relationship builders and can connect with employees, customers, and partners. At the same time, they value accountability and have little tolerance for low performers. According to Rowe, strategic leaders can create the most wealth in their companies through their ability to balance the short-term and long-term strategic requirements and operational performance.

• • •

I love the story of Jan Carlzon, CEO of Scandinavian Airlines (SAS) from 1981 to 1993, and his turnaround of the fast-declining airline in the 1980s.* Jan was a strategic leader, and his commitment to creating a world-class customer experience inspired me to develop the StoneAge Assurance Promise. From its inception until the oil crash in the 1970s, SAS was a profitable airline. The oil bust caught the company off guard, and soon, they were losing money.

With no end in sight due to the stagnation in projected growth, Jan knew he couldn't save his way out of obsolescence; the only way to fix the issue was to grow revenues. But how could he inspire customers to fly SAS? He combined visionary and managerial leadership styles to create a new path forward. He invested his way to growth by clearly defining their target customers: business travelers. Then he spent money on activities that would attract them to SAS. Declaring that SAS would be the best business travel airline in the world was motivating and gave everyone clear direction. In fact, he even wrote *The Little Red Book*, a guide for all employees to help them understand their purpose and the behaviors and attributes that would make them successful at the new SAS. He made tradeoffs such as declining to spend money marketing toward tourists and kept the company focused on attracting and retaining business travelers. And he saved the company.

Put It into Practice:
How to Become a Strategic Leader

While under immense pressure to perform and turn the business around, Jan shifted his approach into strategic leadership; blending both managerial and visionary styles provided him with the sound decision-making and creative thinking needed to navigate out of their difficult circumstance. But strategic leadership is more nuanced than what can be pulled out of a single example.

---

*   Jan Carlzon, *Moments of Truth* (New York: Ballinger, 1989).

considerer long-term and short-term tradeoffs, test your hypothesis, and anticipate the unintended consequences. Then decide.

Align your stakeholders.

Schoemaker, Krupp, and Howland continue, "Strategic leaders must be adept at finding common ground and achieving buy-in among stakeholders who have disparate views and agendas. This requires active outreach. Success depends on proactive communication, trust-building, and frequent engagement." To improve your ability to align the organization, they suggest that you communicate early and often, identify key stakeholders, and anticipate where there might be a misalignment, and look for hidden agendas. Then, facilitate conversations to understand concerns, get buy-in, monitor changing positions, and reward colleagues who support and model alignment.

Learn and grow.

Again, creating a culture of curiosity is key where the organization is encouraged to learn and grow. Strategic leaders study wins and failures with an open mind and transparency to understand what went well and what didn't to make better decisions in the future. To improve your learning ability, create a culture where making mistakes is safe and considered a learning opportunity. Hold after-action reviews to focus on decision-making and analysis, not assigning blame. Document lessons learned and shared them with the team. If something isn't working, fix it or stop doing it.

• • •

Over the last decade, I have developed from being a visionary leader into a strategic one. I am a bit of a risk-taker, and I love ideas. I see endless opportunities, and my natural tendency is to want to go after all of them—at the same time. I am an inspiring communicator. I can rally the troops and get people excited about where we are going as a company. But I have learned the hard way how a vision with no plan can cause confusion and frustration. I have learned how slowing down can allow you to speed up if you use that time to put efficient processes into place. I now see that focus is what creates success and that choosing what opportunities to go after and saying no to all the rest makes a vision achievable. Again, I had to learn this lesson the hard way. And I still must actively work to not let the next shiny object distract me from my mission to disrupt my industry and make, as Steve Jobs so eloquently put, make my dent in the universe.

6

EMBRACE SELF-AWARENESS

Whenever I am asked, "What is the most beneficial quality a leader can have?" I always say, "*Self-awareness and introspection.*" I believe that self-awareness is one of the most underrated but most important qualities *anyone* can have—especially leaders. Self-awareness ensures leaders understand their own strengths as well as limitations. This personal awareness makes leaders more approachable, trustworthy, and successful, because it means they know how to assess their ability to lead in any situation and how to tap others for guidance when their expertise is needed to make decisions.

Looking back on my life, I've always been reasonably self-aware, but I didn't consciously work at it until my early twenties when I was introduced to personality assessments. When I read the assessment results, my good friend and colleague, Paul Reece, taught me about Meyers–Briggs and the light bulbs went off. "Oh my! This is why I do the things I do!" I told Paul as we talked through the various styles. I was hooked after that and began my journey of deeper introspection.

Most of us know that self-awareness is important but don't know where to start or what to do when we realize that we are getting in our own way. Let's start with the fundamentals and then go into the three most important things you can do to develop self-awareness.

What Exactly Is Self-Awareness?

Self-awareness is the ability to look at your actions, words, emotions, and character with clarity and introspection. In 1972, researchers Shelley Duval and Robert Wickland proposed that when a person focuses on their behaviors and decisions and compares them to what they perceive to be the correct way to think, feel, and act, they are more likely to look at themselves and course-correct.* Simply put, self-awareness is the ability to look at yourself to understand what drives your actions and behaviors and then make changes if necessary.

Why Is Self-Awareness Important?

Most of us meander through our days, paying little attention to our actions and decisions. Being on autopilot isn't necessarily bad, as our brain needs to conserve energy for the bigger issues we must tackle in a given day. We get ourselves in trouble when we don't understand how our actions, words, and decisions impact others. That's why developing deep self-awareness is essential. Not only should you be aware of your actions, but you must also understand how they create conflict and drama in your own life and those of others. Even better, deep self-awareness allows you to take ownership of your impact and develop alternative responses and methods to fix the conflict you create.

---

* "Self-Awareness Theory," Ecnyclopedia.com, accessed October 2022, https://www.encyclopedia.com/social-sciences/applied-and-social-sciences-magazines/self-awareness-theory.

Awareness of Blind Spots

We all have blind spots, and they are hard to uncover. Why? Well, because they are *blind spots*. Unidentified blind spots can, at best, hamper good leadership, and at worst, take a leader down. Common blind spots include the need to always be right, blaming others, avoiding confrontation, being a poor listener, and exhibiting insensitivity to how your behavior affects others.

One of the best tools I've seen for helping leaders uncover blind spots is by comparing self-assessment scores with those of a 360-degree assessment given by direct reports, peers, and managers. When there is a gap between how you rate yourself and how others rate you, that's a blind spot.

I had a senior-level manager working for me who was unaware of how his body language, words, and demeanor were affecting his team and peers. After a blow-up in a meeting, I called him into my office and told him he had to change his behavior or he would have to exit the company. He insisted that I was the only one with a problem. "No one gives me negative feedback, and I ask for it all the time! It's only you who has the problem with me," he exclaimed. I explained that no one felt comfortable giving him feedback, and I was the only one being candid because I was his boss—everyone who worked for him was afraid of losing their jobs. I hired a coach to help, and she walked him through the 360-degree process, which revealed several blind spots. It was eye-opening for both of us. He embraced the process and worked hard to understand his blind spots and triggers, modified his behavior, and improved his relationships significantly. I saw the power of candid feedback and deepening self-awareness.

Put It into Practice:
How to Be More Self-Aware

There are many ways to go about developing more awareness, but I have found these three to be especially effective.

Ask for feedback.

Understanding how others perceive you allows you to look at yourself through new eyes. Provided that feedback is given well—meaning constructively and helpfully—you can better understand your strengths and weaknesses. I suggest setting up the feedback this way:

"I am trying to uncover my blind spots to become a more effective leader. Can you help me identify a blind spot that I might have?" Make it safe for the person to give you this kind of feedback.

Explore your motivations.

All humans have intrinsic and extrinsic motivations. *Intrinsic motivations* are those that come from the joy of doing something for the sake of doing it. Examples would be curiosity, purpose, passion, and fun. *Extrinsic motivations* are derived from wanting a specific outcome. Think recognition, promotion, pay raise, winning—or not losing. If you understand your motivations, you can better understand your actions and responses.

Take psychometric assessments.

Using personality and ability assessments is one of the best ways to better understand yourself and uncover blind spots. These assessments measure several attributes, including intelligence, critical thinking, motivation, behavioral patterns, and personality styles. They include assessments such as DISC, Meyers–Briggs, the Enneagram, and the Predictive Index. I highly recommend working with a professional coach when exploring these assessments. A coach can help you better understand what the assessments mean (and don't mean) and can give you tools to successfully navigate your style and modify your behaviors.

Here are some ways that I have used self-awareness to make profound changes in my life:

Example 1

Many people have told me that I seem high-strung. I don't feel like I am, but that's because I don't know how to feel anything different than what I feel and experience. After hearing this a dozen times, I started paying attention to my interactions with others. I realized that when I feel passionate about something, I speak faster and widen my eyes. This is an intense experience for the person I am talking to, but I am caught up in my words and feeling and don't experience myself the same way. To practice more self-awareness, when I start to feel myself amp up, I take a deep breath, smile, and slow down my speaking cadence.

Example 2

I was ecstatic when the Colorado School of Mines accepted me. Although I didn't really understand what an engineer did, nor was I particularly excited about a career as an engineer, I had decided I was going to Mines because it was the hardest school in the state to get into. I wanted to prove to everyone that I was smart enough to be accepted. I worked hard my final two years of high school, turning around my grades to ensure I would be accepted. Paired with winning a scholarship to play softball, it felt like I had made it! *See everyone? I did it! I am a winner!* But because I had decided on attending Mines due to extrinsic motivations, my sense of accomplishment was short-lived. It didn't take me long to figure out that I was not an engineer and being at Mines did not make me happy. I decided to stick with it when faced with continuing or transferring out. Why? I found intrinsic motivation.

This was the beginning of my journey to understand that making decisions based on what others thought of me would lead to poor choices and unhappiness. Although I had to learn this lesson repeatedly over the coming years, I decided to study business economics along with engineering. This was much more in alignment with my curiosity, purpose, and passion. It was incredibly challenging, which I liked because I like to do hard things, and I was doing it for me rather than someone else.

Example 3

I've found the Enneagram to be the most useful personality assessment. The Enneagram is a personality typing system that describes patterns, triggers, emotional responses, and how one manages emotions. There are nine types, and each is defined by a core belief about how the world works. Specifically, I like it because it doesn't leave you feeling like you must "fix yourself." Instead, each type operates in nine levels of health.

Level one is the healthiest, and level nine is the unhealthiest. The purpose of the Enneagram is to help you understand when and why you move into various levels of health. More so than any other assessment, it helped me understand why I do the things I do. I am a Type 3 in the Enneagram, which is the Achiever. Success-oriented, adaptable, driven, and image-conscious. According to the Enneagram Institute, key motivations for Achievers include wanting to distinguish themselves from others, receive attention, be admired, and impress others. Their deepest fear is to be seen as worthless or as a failure.

At their best, Achievers can make a great impact in the world. At their worst, they are deceptive, malicious, vindictive, and selfish. Talk about trigger words. I didn't like these words when I first started digging into my type. But with the help of a brilliant coach, I began to explore my relationship with these words, seeing how they did, in fact, drive my decisions and thought patterns. As I got more comfortable with them, I learned to recognize my patterns and behaviors and make changes to how I was showing up to my team and family. Hands down, working with the Enneagram has helped me develop a deeper sense of myself and others.

• • •

It's difficult to be an impactful leader without self-awareness. When you deepen your self-knowledge, as well as your understanding of others, you gain valuable insight and will be better able to modify your approach to get the results you are looking for. You'll know when you need to apologize or admit a mistake, and you can regulate your emotions, becoming a more predictable and level-headed leader.

7

TAKE FEEDBACK
LIKE A CHAMP

Receiving feedback can be tough, but it's critical in order to grow personally and professionally. How can you improve if you don't know what to improve? And being a leader, there is a good chance you aren't getting feedback. Why? Because you are scary! Even if you aren't, it's human nature to protect oneself, which means giving the boss lip service.

And it's understandable. Many leaders get defensive and make excuses when they get feedback. Reacting in this manner shuts down any curiosity about the shared perspective and is a missed opportunity to grow as a person, better understand your impact on others, and improve your job and relationships. Plus, handling it poorly increases the chance that you won't get honest feedback in the future. Not getting feedback may sound ideal, but it's not. I can guarantee that people have feedback for you, but they don't want to tell you. I don't know about you, but I don't want people telling me what they think I want to hear but feeling or thinking something different.

According to a study done by leadership experts Jack Zenger and Joseph Folkman, the best leaders ask for more feedback. Their research of over 50,000 executives found that "leaders who ranked at the top 10 percent in asking for feedback were rated, on average, at the eighty-sixth percentile in overall leadership effectiveness."* I find this to be true, too. I appreciate the members of my executive team who take feedback well. It's easy to coach and guide them, and I enjoy our candid conversations; they tell me they do, too. I consistently rank these feedback-taking leaders higher than those who get defensive or emotional when receiving feedback. And I work hard to take feedback well, asking for it regularly with an open mind.

I remember the first time I got true "in-your-face" feedback from one of my employees. It was in my second year with the company, and we had just screwed up. I got a call from an angry customer telling me that we sent him a used product. A *very expensive* used product. *What? How could this be?* I asked him to send me pictures, and when I received them, he was right; there was rust on the steel and dings in the paint.

I immediately went to my shop and demanded to know what had happened. In front of the entire team, including our sales manager, I asked, "How could you have sent this overseas to one of our most important customers?" They looked at me nervously, eyes wide but silent.

"There is no way we sent it like that," my shop manager said. "Something must have happened while it was with the cargo carrier. Or the customer is lying."

I felt my face flush. *How is he not taking any responsibility for this? Really? He's blaming the customer?* I replied, "Well, I don't care how it happened. It's your problem, and you need to fix it. Make sure this

* Jack Craven, "Being a Great Leader Means Giving and Receiving Feedback," *Forbes*, January 16, 2018, https://www.forbes.com/sites/forbescoachescouncil/2018/01/16/being-a-great-leader-means-giving-and-receiving-feedback/?sh=1f592cebc905.

explanation, justification, and excuse-making. Tread carefully here. Sometimes, it's best to say thank you and incorporate the feedback into your work or life without offering justification for your actions or behaviors. Interjecting with excuses is a sure-fire way to be labeled as unaccountable.

Ask for time to process.

If I feel myself getting defensive and I can't get it under control with a few deep breaths, I say, "This is a lot for me to process right now. May I have a bit of time to think about what you are saying and come back later to talk through it?" Most people need time to process feedback, and it's entirely reasonable to ask for space to think. Plus, taking some time to ponder the feedback can help you assess its validity. Just make sure you set a time to circle back. You don't want to blow off the person brave enough to share constructive criticism. Have an open mind and heart and resist the urge to defend yourself.

Pay attention.

After receiving feedback, I try to be hyper-mindful of exhibiting the behaviors brought to my attention. There are always opportunities to *stop doing* or *start doing* the critiqued conduct. For example, if you were told you interrupt people, pay close attention to yourself when conversing with others. Notice when you find yourself wanting to interject. How do you feel, and why do you want to add your two cents? Were you able to stop yourself? If not, did you take accountability for interrupting and apologize? Being mindful and making in-the-moment course corrections are great ways to improve.

• • •

I work hard at being coachable and approachable and at taking feedback with grace. It's not always easy, and I certainly have screwed up my share of conversations because I let myself get defensive. But I've gotten better at it because I'm committed to growth and development as a person and leader. Just like any skill, you have to practice getting better at it. Looking back over the constructive criticism I've received, I am incredibly grateful for the people who have cared enough to share it with me. Each time, they have offered me a golden opportunity to take steps toward becoming the person I want to be. To all of you, I say, "Thank you for the feedback."

8

GET A COACH

One of the top investments you can make in yourself is to hire a coach. Seriously—find a way to fit the cost into your budget. It doesn't matter what type of leadership role you are in; there are all kinds of personal development and life coaches who specialize in various types of clients. You can find one who will fit your needs no matter where you are in your career or personal life. I promise you won't regret it.

A 2008 study published in *The Consulting Psychology Journal* found that executive coaching *works*. The study authors found that coaching affected positive change in five key areas: people management, relationship with managers, goal setting and prioritization, engagement and productivity, and dialogue and communication.[*] Over 70 percent of the executives in the study said that coaching increased their confidence. Over 80 percent said that coaching improved their effectiveness and had an overall positive impact on their businesses. These executives found

---

[*] Francis A. Kombarakaran, Julia A. Yang, Mila N. Baker, and Pauline B. Fernandes, "Executive Coaching: It Works!" *Consulting Psychology Journal: Practice & Research* 60, no. 1 (2008): 78–90.

that they became better people managers, increased their self-awareness, listened more deeply, and asked better questions.

According to the study, "executives increased their people effectiveness by building on strengths and working through their blind spots; strengthened their relationships with their managers, direct reports, and others; and developed the skills and experience to coach others. Executive coaching assisted in attaining a higher level of executive performance. A well-designed coaching program with external coaches can help executives with transitions, as demonstrated in this study. Factors in the success of this executive coaching engagement included: the selection of good coaches, good environmental program support, executive commitment, and the participation of managers. Executives gained new perspectives and practice new behavioral approaches that led to executive change and increased strategic leadership."

I started working with coaches early in my days as CEO and continue to do so. There is no doubt that I have benefited greatly from it. In the beginning, my goal was to find a coach who could help me understand myself better and grow as a leader. I needed someone I could bounce ideas off of. Someone I could say anything to without fear of being judged as emotional, irrational, or flat-out wrong. Someone to whom I could say: "I don't know how to handle this situation." I was looking for someone who would help me hold myself accountable and teach me new tools for handling challenging situations.

My first coach was a combination business and life coach who worked with the Enneagram. I was nervous to begin my work with her, as I was unsure of what I would learn about myself. But I knew I needed help unpacking the issues that lead me to self-hatred, loneliness, and eventually addiction. I had been to a therapist, but I didn't find it effective. I could talk about my feelings, but my therapist didn't provide a framework to help me understand my personality and impulses. Plus, I was early in my leadership journey at StoneAge, and I wanted to invest in myself, hoping that I would learn how to be a more effective leader in a shorter amount of time. I chose a life coach for a few reasons. First, the coach I selected was the first coach I had ever met, and I didn't know the difference between life and executive coaching. Second, I clicked with her. Her approach was intriguing, and I was curious about the Enneagram. She helped me understand my desire for recognition and deeply self-reflect and modify my style to benefit others without losing my authenticity, which is my most important value.

Later, I began working with more business-focused coaches who helped me create a comprehensive, disciplined management system that was well suited for my style. I experienced the same improvements as the executives in the study: improved relationships that increased engagement across the organization, the ability to set better goals and prioritize in a way that allowed up to execute our strategy better, and deeper self-awareness that allowed me to show up authentically, vulnerably, and with the grit needed to run a dynamic, growing organization in today's challenging environment.

I appreciate the relationship I have with my current coach, who is a former CEO and knows exactly what kind of pressure I am under. He is helping me build my plan to scale StoneAge into a billion-dollar organization, keeping me focused and accountable to working on high-value activities that will move the company forward. He's a confidant and sounding board, which is helpful in the lonely world of executive leadership.

Coaching has been so impactful that I hired the first coach I ever worked with, the life coach, to work with my employees. She has developed a six-month deep coaching program that dozens of my employees have gone through. The results are remarkable; everyone who has gone through her program reports a deeper understanding of themselves and others and gains valuable tools to navigate their stress. Coaching has helped them embrace the ownership mindset.

Put It into Practice: What Coaches Can Do for You

Provide unbiased listening.

There is great benefit in talking with someone who isn't attached to you or your situation. Even if those closest to you are great listeners, they are still impacted by what you say and do and cannot be completely unbiased. A coach is there to support you and only you and will listen and give feedback accordingly. Talk to your coach about the good, bad, and the ugly. Don't hold back; if you do, you won't get the most out of your coaching relationship.

Extend candid feedback.

Candid feedback is a gift, even if it sometimes hurts. Unfortunately, it's rare to get direct, constructive criticism and advice. As you move toward higher levels of management, getting feedback becomes even more important. Unfortunately, you're less likely to get it, and if you do, it's probably not accurate (face it, most people are too scared to tell the boss what they *really* think). A good coach will give it to you straight. In fact, some of the toughest feedback I've ever received was from one of my coaches. At first, I was angry with her, but when I realized that she was simply holding up a mirror for me to look in, I understood what she was saying and was able to own my behavior and choices. Receiving this kind of feedback can help you change your life and leadership—if you are willing to hear it.

9

BELIEVE IN YOURSELF

Several years back, I met with a customer who told me that he was surprised the founders of StoneAge hired me to take over the company. "I don't think you'll make it," he said. "This is too tough of a business for someone who isn't technical and doesn't have field experience." In other words: "You'll never make it in this industry because you are a woman." This statement stuck with me for quite some time. I heard the same thing from a previous boss and walked away from the company to prove that I could sell a technical product. This time, his words made me question my talent and ability because I was in a new role that challenged me daily. I began to doubt myself. *Am I able to do this job well? Maybe I'm not technical enough. What if our customers shun me?* were all thoughts that ran through my head.

I talked about it often with people close to me, until one day a friend said to me, "You have clearly done a good job. Look at where the company is now. You need to forget what he said and move on." My friend was right. I was holding onto an insensitive comment. It weighed on my confidence and was not serving me. The comment just didn't matter.

We all must overcome doubts and doubters. Well-meaning people often try to talk you out of following your dreams. "It's just too risky," they say. Ignore them and stay true to yourself. If we don't take ownership of our own truth, our own identity, someone else will own it for us—and that never results in fulfillment. I think back to my dad telling me I wasn't smart enough to graduate from engineering school. Even though I lost myself along the way, the Colorado School of Mines opened so many doors for me, and I am glad I persevered. The same goes for comments on not being technical enough, skinny enough, pretty enough, and having enough experience. Looking back on all that I had overcome, I finally said to myself, *Hey, if I am going to believe in something, it might as well be myself.*

Self-doubt is inevitable, and it can actually be a good thing—in moderation. Self-doubt creeps in when we try new things and aren't sure how they will turn out. It shows up when we care about our work and our relationships. It's useful when it motivates us to learn, practice, and take action. But self-doubt is paralyzing when it takes over, derailing us from our goals because we fear failure or rejection. Success is dependent on our ability to keep this inevitability in check

According to Nick Wignall, a clinical psychologist based in Albuquerque, New Mexico, there are three main types of self-doubt.

Imposter Syndrome

"Imposter syndrome is the irrational fear of being a fraud or not deserving of your accomplishments," says Wignall. There have been many times that I have felt this way. Throughout my career, I've had times when I thought, *I have no idea what I am doing. What if someone finds out?* I have questioned if I have what it takes to be a CEO. In fact, after receiving a snarky comment from a direct report who said, "You

We all are enough; we just have to believe it. And when the doubts creep in, and assuredly they will, we must examine where they come from and keep moving forward.

Put It into Practice: How to Get Over Self-Doubt

When self-doubt bubbles up inside of me, here are some things I do to use it as a superpower rather than let it immobilize me.

Ask yourself two questions.

These are the first two questions I ask myself when I'm filled with doubt: *What's the worst that can happen? What's the best thing that could happen?* Why? Because these questions help put things in perspective and give opposing outcomes at opposite ends of the spectrum. When I started my podcast, *Reflect Forward*, I was scared and had all kinds of doubts. So, I asked myself these two questions. My answers: *The worst thing that could happen is that no one listens to it because it's not well marketed. The best thing that could happen is that people love it, and it becomes a popular business podcast that helps people become better leaders.*

I decided that it wouldn't be that bad if no one listened to it; I would stop recording and move on to something different. But when I thought about the possibility of it being received well, I was motivated by the thought of making an impact through my podcast. I decided to listen to dozens of business podcasts and take notes on what I liked and didn't like. And that's how I created my show. While it's not wildly popular (yet), it's gaining traction, moving up in the ratings, and I'm growing a following. And most importantly, I find tremendous joy in creating my weekly podcasts.

Talk to someone.

We all tell ourselves stories about why we will fail, why people don't like us, and why we aren't worthy of success. Usually, these stories are distorted, exaggerated, and out of touch with reality; we rarely tell ourselves stories with positive outcomes. Talking to someone helps. Not only does it feel good to get your self-doubts out in the open but talking to someone who believes in you can give you a new perspective. Plus, you are more likely to realize how exaggerated your thoughts have become when you say things out loud.

I did this when I was told I wasn't disruptive but erratic instead. I vented to my husband, expressing worry that I didn't have what it takes to be a CEO. "Maybe I shouldn't do this anymore," I said to him. "I suck at being a CEO." He laughed, which wasn't helpful, but then he said, "You are an incredibly talented CEO. People are inspired by your leadership every day. Do you do everything perfectly? No. But you do not suck at being a CEO, and that laugh was meant to get a rise out of you." Ryan was right. He helped me see I was being irrational and gave me good advice. "Sleep on it," he said, "and if you still want to give up in the morning, we will devise a plan." He knows me too well—there was no way I was giving up, and I jumped out of bed the next morning holding a new appreciation for my job.

Consider the past.

The past can be a powerful teacher if we pause to analyze the outcomes of various situations and decisions. Whenever I have self-doubts, I look to the past and consider how things turned out, what decisions I made, what I would do differently, and what I wouldn't change. Building upon past successes and overcoming failure gives me the courage to push self-doubt aside and move forward. Every time I feel like I can't do something, I think about lying on the floor of my apartment all those years ago, willing myself not to die. If I could pick myself up off the floor and create a whole new life, I can overcome the challenge now in front of me.

Take action, even if it's small.

I firmly believe that taking action is the fastest way to overcome your fears. When I am filled with self-doubt, I go for a walk and ponder why I feel stuck and insecure. I think about what I could do to get unstuck. Almost always, a few ideas pop up organically. Then I choose one of these ideas and act on it. Just one small step forward. Getting unstuck isn't easy, but it is simple. You have to move. You have to decide. You have to act. And you need to do it sooner than later; inertia isn't easy to overcome, and it's easy to talk yourself out of taking that one small step if you wait too long.

Remember, no one is really paying attention.

The uncomfortable truth is that no one pays that much attention to what we say and do. It may feel like the spotlight is on you, but in reality, most people are too busy thinking about their own problems, hopes, dreams, fears, and self-doubts. I often remind myself: *You are not the center of anyone's universe but your own. Just take action and stop worrying about what other people think. They probably aren't thinking about you anyway.* This reminder helps me get over myself and take that small step.

I love what Kara Goldin, founder of Hint Water, says in her book, *Undaunted: Overcoming Doubts and Doubters*: "We can't change the way of the world. What we can do is look our doubt and our doubters in the eye and refuse to be stopped by them. It's not about high IQ, elite credentials, super skills, or any of those other traits we often convince ourselves we must have but are afraid we don't."

Embrace imposter syndrome.

Until recently, imposter syndrome has been considered a debilitating trait. While I agree that believing you are unworthy of your accomplishments diminishes self-confidence and adds more pressure to perform, embracing imposter syndrome can help you perform better. A recent study conducted by Basima Tewfik, assistant professor of Work and Organization Studies at the Massachusetts Institute of Technology, found that the syndrome often paid off. She discovered that professionals across a wide range of industries who had self-doubt were more empathetic, asked better questions, were better listeners, had higher-rated interpersonal skills, and were more collaborative than their non-imposter colleagues.

"A lot of people sort of paint [imposter syndrome] as this thing that's holding you back. So, we would expect, for example, that maybe you'd be a poor performer," says Tewfik. "There's actually no significant difference [in competence] between those who are induced to have imposter thoughts and those who are not."

Looking back on how I went from rock bottom to a successful CEO in a few short years, I realized that I leaned into my self-doubt. I acknowledged what I didn't know, and I asked a million questions. Sure, the fears in the back of my mind whispered to me that I wasn't cut out to be a CEO or that the mistakes I made would get me fired for incompetence due to lack of experience, but I used what I didn't know as fuel. Fuel to learn, create deeper competency, communicate more clearly, and lead with curiosity.

• • •

Remember, you aren't alone. Even former first lady Michelle Obama acknowledged imposter syndrome. In her best-selling book *Becoming*, she wrote, "I still have a little impostor syndrome . . . It doesn't go away, that feeling that you shouldn't take me that seriously. What do I know? I share that with you because we all have doubts in our abilities, about our power and what that power is." And my advice to you is: don't let self-doubt take away your power; instead, use it to propel you forward.

10

BE HUMBLE

Humility matters, perhaps more so today than ever. When exhibited regularly and authentically, humility is a character trait that can help us be better listeners, inspire others, build relationships, and give us insight into different ways of thinking and being—something that, in my opinion, we are in desperate need of. The only way we can solve the massive issues we face as a society is to be humbler in leading, following, thinking, speaking, and acting.

In contrast, arrogance—humility's antithesis—happens when we let our egos get in our way. Arrogance is the gateway to intolerance, exclusion, and judgmental mindsets. It is the killer of curiosity because it leads to thinking, *I know what's right. I know what's wrong. I know what's best. I don't care what you think.* It allows us to tell ourselves that we can say and do whatever we want with little regard for others: screw political correctness, general cordialness, or respectful debate. In fact, let's just go to war and impose our will. This mindset is incredibly dangerous and obviously unproductive, given the state of the world right now.

So, what exactly is humility? *Merriam-Webster* defines it as "the quality or state of not thinking you are better than other people." C. S. Lewis says it's "not thinking less of yourself; it's thinking of yourself less." The Urban Dictionary states it is "remaining teachable, knowing that you do not have all the answers."

As a young but driven CEO, I learned this lesson the hard way, especially being a person who values words of affirmation and likes to be publicly recognized. My ego can get the better of me when not kept in check. I recall a very humbling moment early in my CEO tenure when my executive coach told me, "You use the word 'I' far too often." It felt harsh at the moment; I absolutely believed that I was successful only because I was part of a great team and had a strong support system that helped me when I found myself in over my head. But maybe I wasn't showing it.

I began to pay attention to my words, and sure enough, I found myself saying "I" all the time. It was subconscious but present, probably due to my need to receive recognition to feel worthy. I decided to dig into this deeply felt need, exploring why it kept tripping me up. My relationship with my father was traumatic and played into my wanting recognition, but my personality also plays into it heavily. I could see these patterns in my past, especially when I got caught up in addiction. Not wanting to use my personality as an excuse, I decided that finding balance was worth the effort. I could be self-confident *and* humble. I could be a leader *and* a follower. I could be recognized while letting others shine, too.

I am an avid reader, and I enjoy reading books by other CEOs. I am always hit with a twinge of guilt when I read words like Hubert Joly, former CEO of Best Buy, wrote in his book *The Heart of Business: Leadership Principles for the Next Era of Capitalism*: "As CEO, I deliberately kept a low profile, turning down most requests to appear on TV shows and the covers of magazines. To me, management is not about the fame and glory of being a CEO; it's about the work and the people I was there to lead and inspire."

Statements like these make me question if I enjoy the spotlight too much. I fully agree that my job is to do the hard work of leading and inspiring, but is it wrong to accept interviews and promote myself and my company? Would I be a better leader if I led from the back, stayed behind the scenes, and kept my head down? But I always come back to the importance of staying true to myself. Authenticity matters and I am passionate about driving change, disrupting the way we think about business and leadership. I want to help other leaders find their way to being exceptional. It's hard not to compare yourself to other successful leaders, but the truth is, there is no one way to do things. We all have to find what works for us. What works for me is publicly pushing boundaries, speaking up for what I believe in, and sharing my experiences to inspire others to embrace their flaws and step fully into the beautiful messiness of leadership. But even though we're confident in the approaches that work for us, it doesn't mean we all shouldn't approach leadership with humility.

All leaders need to stay grounded, but it's not always easy. Here are some ways I stay humble, and I offer them as suggestions for you, too.

Put It into Practice: How to Be a Humble Leader

Understand yourself.

We all have talents and strengths; we all have faults and weaknesses. Having a deep understanding of yours will help you stay grounded. When you judge others for their shortcomings, remember that you, too, have qualities that can negatively affect your relationships and decrease your overall effectiveness. Make a commitment to yourself and those close to you to stay open to learning and understanding the blind spots you have that might not be so flattering. Focus on improving yourself rather than condemning others.

Don't showboat or brag.

Self-confidence is important, but no one wants to hear about how great you are at this or that, nor do they care about your golf handicap, what kind of car you drive, or how big your house is. When acknowledgement is your love language, it can be difficult, at first, to refrain from oversharing accomplishments or status. When unsure of how you may come across, consider if what you're about to add to the conversation genuinely adds substance to your conversation or relationship. If the answer is no, keep the comments to yourself.

Admit when you are wrong, make a mistake, have poor judgment, or fumble a situation.

Acknowledging when we've slipped up or underperformed is tough. When you care about something deeply, admitting failure or a mistake can grate on your confidence. No one is perfect, and you shouldn't pretend to be. In fact, most people value this kind of authenticity and vulnerability. Don't be afraid to admit your mistakes and own your actions. Although your ego may try to convince you otherwise, this transparency and groundedness will make you a better leader.

Apologize when you need to, and sometimes even when you don't.

An apology says, "I understand I had a role in this and am accountable for it." And it makes space for others to do the same. Great leaders don't hesitate to apologize when they've made mistakes or hurt others unintentionally. It is important to apologize straightforwardly, without folding any nuanced language in that points fingers back at the other person. True ownership and leadership exhibits confidence and understanding even when we are admitting we've done something we wished we hadn't.

Show gratitude and give credit to others.

Yes, you have worked hard for what you have, but you wouldn't be where you are today if it weren't for all the people who supported you along the way. Say thank you and be appreciative of what you have and of those who've helped you. Show others that you value their talents, qualities, and viewpoints. Surround yourself with people who are different than you and appreciate what they bring to the relationship. Defer to others' judgment. Ask them for their opinions and feedback. Say thank you often.

Be a constant learner.

As Aristotle said, "The more you know, the more you know you don't know." There's almost nothing more humbling than recognizing that you contain a fraction of all knowledge available. So, commit to learning more. Don't limit yourself to what's in books or on the news. Learn about your community, other people, contrasting viewpoints, and different cultures. Ask a lot of questions and be curious for the sake of learning, not for building your case as to why you are right. Understand that the learning process will never be over for you, and that's a good thing.

Help others, no matter the situation, and don't be afraid to ask for help yourself.

Everyone needs help at some point in their lives. Don't judge or condemn those less fortunate or with bigger problems than you. Treat them as equals—as fellow human beings—because it's the right thing to do. The people I trusted and leaned on while recovering from my addiction didn't ask me demeaning questions or assume I'd fail. They lifted me up so I could heal and recover and go on to accomplish great things and help others. You don't have to go it alone. Asking for help doesn't show weakness. It shows that you are humble enough to recognize when you need it and have the courage to ask.

• • •

I'll leave you with another quote, this time from Gordon B. Hinckley, who so eloquently said, "Being humble means recognizing that we are not on earth to see how important we can become but to see how much difference we can make in the lives of others." What would our lives, our communities, and the world be like if we all believed in and lived by this mantra—not just for those we know and love, but for all of humanity?

11

OVERCOME YOUR FEAR OF BEING DISLIKED

I know I am not supposed to say this, but I'm going to anyway: I want to be liked as a leader. Can you believe I just admitted that? I don't know how often I've heard people say that you must get over the need to be liked as a leader. Logically, I believe these words, or that at the very least, you must find ways to care less about being liked. Emotionally, though, it's hard to turn off such an innate desire. Being liked gives a sense of belonging and inclusion, two things most of us crave.

A few years ago, I discussed my want to be liked with one of my executive team members, and he said something interesting. He believed that a person's desire to be liked would lead him or her down the path to inauthenticity. He questioned, "If you have such a strong desire to be liked, how can you make the tough decisions, have the hard conversations, and be authentic in the face of a storm? How do you overcome the need to be liked and make hard decisions that might make some people *not* like you?"

What great questions. I thought long and hard about the viewpoint and could see myself in his questioning. I certainly avoided some tough conversations because I didn't want a person to be mad at me. Early in my days as CEO, I had even sugarcoated tough feedback to this same employee who gave me this current feedback because I wanted him to like me. But what I learned from this experience was that I often confused being *respected* with being *liked*. As I matured as a leader, I found that being liked became less important than being respected. That being said, I believe that likeability matters, and the key is finding the balance.

Let's first establish that to be a good leader, you do not have to be liked. To be a good leader, you must be well respected and credible, which you gain through making good decisions; admitting mistakes; being honest, genuine, and self-aware; communicating regularly and clearly; and living and breathing your purpose. These traits describe authenticity, and being an authentic leader is not only the best way to lead. It's the only way to lead.

But in my experience, being liked by those you lead is helpful, and it brings a sense of fulfillment. When people like you, they want to be around you. They are more likely to ask your opinion and give their opinions. They feel more comfortable being vulnerable, making it easier and more fun to partner with you to get things done. When you are liked, it's easier to influence your desired outcomes because people genuinely engage with you and want to help.

After thinking long and hard about this, I believe that being liked, authentic, and respected plays a significant part in taking ownership as a leader.

Being an authentic leader must always come first. Likeability should be lower on the list but not dismissed entirely. Although likeability is not as imperative as respect, likeability allows leaders to connect with their teams on a human level. Great leaders know how to blend these two components to maximize effectiveness. Learn to be okay with making decisions that not everyone will like; doing the right thing is always more important than making everyone happy. That being said, make sure you explain the *why* behind your decisions (refer to chapter 26, which explains how to do this effectively); bringing people along for the ride will create loyalty and trust. Don't be afraid to have a hard conversation; people want to know where they stand.

When you coach and guide rather than avoid or criticize, you help people develop their professional and interpersonal skills. Be direct but do it with kindness and respect. Consider how you want people to feel when they leave your presence: empowered and believed in or reprimanded and insecure? Be open and share things about yourself; allow people to connect with who you are. A little bit of vulnerability and humility will go a long way in building lasting relationships with people who respect and like you.

Put It into Practice: How to Get Over Your Need to Be Liked

Put it into perspective.

There are over eight billion people on this earth. Not all of them will like you. Only a tiny fraction will ever know you. So why are you worried about pleasing everyone, hoping they like you? Do you like everyone? No! You click with some and not with others. When you don't like someone, how much does it actually impact your life? Probably very little. Well, that's how people who don't like you feel, too. So quit worrying about it and lead.

Recognize that being inauthentic backfires.

People will eventually notice and wind up shunning you when you show up as a less-than-true version of yourself. Why? Because people won't trust you to be honest. People won't know who you truly are, and they might feel manipulated. Eventually, they will disregard you or avoid you. If you want people to like you, don't pretend to be someone you aren't. Be authentic, honest, and share your thoughts. Ask for feedback and course-correct when necessary.

Get clear on what you want.

Many leaders confuse being liked with being respected. They are different. Start by asking yourself, *What do I want out of my work and work relationships?* I believe most of us would answer, *To be respected, trusted, and seen as competent.* If that's the case, you must do things that create respect, trust, and competency. That means being kind yet direct, giving feedback, sharing your opinions, making hard-but-good decisions, and admitting when you are wrong.

Trust yourself.

You can't make everyone happy. And you'll no doubt screw up, make a poor decision, or stick your foot in your mouth. That's okay, so has everyone else. Trust that you'll make good decisions with good intentions. Trust that if you make a mistake, you'll own it and fix it. Trust that when you have a challenging conversation, you'll do it in a way that builds the relationship.

Remember that disagreeing is not the same as being disliked.

This was a huge one for me. I always equated agreement with likeability. I've learned that very few people agree with everything I say and think but that they still respect, like, and follow my lead. It's the same for you. Encourage disagreement, be curious about differing points of view, respectfully debate ideas, listen, and adjust your thinking when wrong. Be okay with disagreeing, and you'll find that people will respect you and even like you more for it!

• • •

On this wonderfully intense, profoundly life-changing leadership journey, I've developed a thicker skin, and I care a little bit less about being liked, but the likable need still sits close to the surface. And for that, I am glad. My desire to connect with those I lead means that I am more thoughtful about my decisions and conversations because I recognize that what I say and do can profoundly impact those around me. It helps me put myself in others' shoes and see things from different points of view. It helps me lead with compassion and empathy. And when I must make a tough decision that some may not like, or if I deliver a message that strikes an emotional chord, I am grateful for the feeling of discomfort it brings because it means I care, I'm invested, and I'm human. It creates more opportunities to pause and reflect, asking myself and those I lead if I could have done it better. To me, all of this is what being authentic is about. And never does the desire to be liked eclipse the desire to be authentic.

12

MAKE TIME TO THINK

Whether you are a leader, manager, or employee who wants to be a high performer, there is almost nothing more important than creating more time to think. It may seem next to impossible in this fast-paced, constantly-plugged-in world, but it *must* be a priority if personal and professional growth is important to you. Why? Because if you aren't making time to think through problems, the future, and your role in what comes next, you will always be reacting. If you constantly react, you aren't giving yourself time to see the possibilities, think through potential consequences, calm down, and ultimately make better decisions.

I don't know about you, but I like making good decisions.

This type of thinking is also called "slow thinking." In his book, *Thinking, Fast and Slow*, Nobel Prize winner Daniel Kahneman hypothesizes that our brains process information in two ways: fast thinking and slow thinking.* Fast thinking is instinctive and automatic. It's the thoughts that seem to appear out of nowhere. It's your gut telling you what to do,

---

* Daniel Kahneman, *Thinking, Fast and Slow* (New York: Farrar, Straus and Giroux, 2013).

which is good in the case of breathing and not so good when we jump to conclusions. Slow thinking is more deliberate, requiring "attention to the effortful mental activities that demand it, including complex computations." You use slow thinking when you need to pay close attention to what's happening around you. You need it to solve hard problems, debate ideas, and to control your responses in high-stakes situations.

Growing up with the business, I found it difficult to pull myself out of the day-to-day operations, even as I matured into my CEO role. I found my days were filled with meetings that I didn't need to be in, but I didn't know how to let go. After receiving some feedback from my board about my lack of a clearly articulated vision for the company, I knew I had to make changes. I was so busy working *in* the business that I didn't have time to work *on* the business. In fact, I didn't know what "working on the business" even meant.

I met with my executive team to ask their opinions. They agreed with the board: I was too involved in the day-to-day, and I needed to think about our growth plan and ensure that we all knew where we were going as a company. So we came up with a process that would allow me to forego meetings but still be informed of important details that allowed me to monitor the health of decisions and the overall organization.

For several hours each day over the following month, I spent time reading, thinking, and writing. I would go for a run or a mountain bike ride and either listen to business books or let my mind wander. Soon, I could see the vision, and I articulated our plan. I came up with new ideas for building my team and the overall company culture. I found a love for writing and started my blog, which was simply a documentation of my actions to grow the company.

After presenting my vision for the future to the board, one member pulled me aside and said, "See, now you are thinking and acting like a CEO. Great job. Keep it up."

Put It into Practice:
Make More Time to Think

Respond instead of reacting.

First, let's consider why responding is so much better than reacting. When you find yourself in a situation where you must react, fight-or-flight mode kicks in. Stress hormones wash through your body, and you feel compelled to say or do something that you may later regret. Reacting is a natural urge; it happens automatically, and it must be consciously resisted. Instead of reacting, choose to respond. You can do this by taking a breath (literally) and giving yourself time to reflect on what's happening at the moment. This pause can be a few seconds, a few minutes, or a few days, and it will allow you to observe what's going on inside and out, making it easier to gain control of your emotions and decision-making process.

Stop wasting so much time.

Social media, news feeds, television, and other distractions should be reduced to a minimum if you want to create more time to think. These things divert precious time and create background noise that clogs your thinking. Do you do anything with the steady stream of content that comes from these sources anyway? When was the last time you had a profound, life-changing realization from a tweet or an Instagram post? Never? Me neither. Close those apps and fill your newfound time with things like reading thought-provoking books and articles, writing out your vision, thinking about how to achieve your goals, and brainstorming ways to improve your relationships. There are so many meaty topics to think about—things that could change your life—if you only allow yourself time to stop and think about them.

Simplify your schedule.

"The difference between successful people and really successful people is that really successful people say no to almost everything." This quote by Warren Buffet pretty much sums it up. The busier you are, the less time you have to think. The less time you have to think, the harder it is to be really successful. Buffet continues, "I insist on a lot of time being spent, almost every day, to just sit and think." It's hard to argue with one of the most successful people on the planet. Simplifying will help you focus on what's most important.

Try this exercise: Write down all the things you feel are priorities in these categories—work, family, personal wellness/fulfillment. List at least twenty items in each category. Then force yourself to pick the top three in each category. Don't do anything else but these nine things until you've mastered them. Now that's simplifying! Focus is the key to success.

Delegate necessary tasks.

Another way of simplifying your life is to delegate. Are you *the* person who *must* do all the tasks on your list? Hire someone to clean your house; have groceries delivered to your door; make your kids ride the bus to school; ask a coworker to help you with a task; approach your boss about getting administrative support on a big project. If you are a manager or a leader, make sure you hire people you can delegate to and empower them to take on challenging assignments. Give them projects that you might typically do yourself. When you find yourself performing tasks that are in the weeds, ask yourself, *Should I be doing this or managing this?* If the answer is managing it, delegate it.

Get organized.

Being disorganized is a time suck. Plan your day so you don't waste time looking for items that should be handy, doing things twice, and working on unimportant tasks. Be disciplined; make a daily schedule that lines out your day. This list shouldn't be too long and should include a block of time to think and the three things you must do to move the ball down the field on your most important priorities. I track my tasks in a project management software called Asana, but any note-taking system will do.

Take a lunch break.

Resist the temptation to work while you scarf down a sandwich; lunchtime is the perfect time to ponder. Step away from your desk and breathe deeply. Jot down new ideas in a notebook; reflect on your day and develop ways to do things better; consider what you might be missing when tackling a big problem at home or work. Better yet, take a walk and let your mind wander; be curious as to where your thoughts take you. Use these thirty minutes to get away from the grind and think.

Find your method.

There are lots of different ways to do your best thinking. Mine happens when I am exercising. The trouble is that I forget everything as soon as I stop; therefore, I use note-taking and audio recording apps to capture ideas as I work out. Pausing to type out a few ideas during a run isn't ideal, but it works for me. I also frequently read and listen to audiobooks, and I use the same apps to record ideas sparked from consuming thought-provoking content. Writing is an excellent outlet for expressing an idea to a colleague via email, journaling, outlining your thoughts on paper, or writing a draft memo to your boss. Other people do their best thinking in the shower, while walking the dog, during long flights, or lying on the beach starting at the ocean. Find what works best for you and do it as often as possible. The outcome will be better decisions, more intentional responses, and a clearer pathway to a fulfilling life.

• • •

Making time to think might just be the most important thing you can do as a leader. It may feel odd at first as you shift away from always "doing," but let go of the guilty feelings, as they won't serve you. It's your job to think about how to grow your team and company. Creating space to think will lead to more clarity and better outcomes.

13

QUESTION
YOUR THOUGHTS

Have you ever stopped to question your thoughts? Where did this thought come from? Why do I think this way? Is this thought even true? It's a powerful moment when you wake up and realize that the way you think might not be the truth. In fact, it's probably *not* the truth.

Here is a perspective for you to ponder: As you read this book, thoughts and opinions about it pop into your head. You love it, it resonates with you, and you can grab hold of something and take action right now. Those thoughts are based on your experiences, preferences, judgments, emotions, and most likely your feelings about me as a person and leader, even if you've never met me.

Someone else reading my book is having a completely different experience. She hates it, thinks I am writing nonsense, and can't find anything in it worth trying to implement. She wonders why anyone would publish me or hire me to speak on leadership.

Both experiences feel like the truth to each person, but whose truth is right? The answer is *neither and both.*

We live in an age where we tell ourselves that being *right* is worth fighting and even killing for and where tolerance, acceptance, compromise, and admitting that you are wrong are signs of weakness. But here's the kicker: *we are never right, because there is no absolute right way.* There are eight billion people on this earth, which means there are eight billion different ways to think about everything there is to be thought about. That's mind-blowing. If there are eight billion different ways to think about the thought you just had, how can you be so sure that the way you think is the truth?

Questioning your thoughts is extremely powerful and brings true self-awareness. Yes, it can create discomfort, especially when challenging your belief systems, but it's also eye-opening and life-changing. Not believing that your thoughts are always true—that your way is the only way—can lead you to new perspectives, to new ways of thinking, to stretch yourself, and (most importantly as a leader) to make better decisions. Not believing everything you think allows you to make room for other people's ideas and solutions. It cultivates tolerance, acceptance, and compromise. It helps you be a better person, parent, and leader.

According to Peter Jansen, emotional intelligence and leadership coach, "As leaders, we guide people, companies, organizations, countries, and even civilization through change. We have the responsibility to have a vision and to influence others. Conveying your vision requires the use of clear, focused, inspired language, and influencing others can only be done through empathy. The magic in language comes from our imagination. When words enter our minds, our imaginations form stories, timelines, and narratives, and these shape us."*

---

* Peter Jansen, "Develop the Quality of Your Thoughts to Shape the Quality of Your Leadership," *Forbes*, April 2, 2019, https://www.forbes.com/sites/forbescoachescouncil/2019/04/02/develop-the-quality-of-your-thoughts-to-shape-the-quality-of-your-leadership/?sh=6f14f2f93324.

Recently, I was forced to challenge my thinking during an in-depth interview process. Interviewing candidates is hard, especially for key positions. I have made mistakes in the past, so when I hired StoneAge's first corporate counsel, I wanted to get it right. We have a very in-depth interview process that involves a broad set of stakeholders in various roles within the company. After an exhaustive set of interviews, the pool of candidates narrowed to three. And the interview team wasn't in alignment. One candidate everyone loved, but I didn't connect with her. I had a funny gut feeling—something was off. My second-choice candidate was everyone else's third choice—even a hard "no" for a few. But I saw something in her, a diamond in the rough. I saw a little bit of myself in her at that age.

I spent a weekend ruminating over the hiring decision, challenging myself and considering my biases. It's common advice to "leave your gut out of hiring decisions," but I don't subscribe to this line of thought, at least not entirely. I have made bad decisions when I have gone with and against my gut, and I know that sometimes I get it right, and sometimes I get it wrong.

I questioned what I was thinking and my reliance on gut feeling. *Am I being unfair to the woman I didn't connect with because I am rooting for the underdog, the woman who reminds me of me when I struggled to figure out what I wanted to do with my life? Should I trust my gut or go with the team? Is my gut right? Why am I feeling this way? How can I figure this out?*

The only way to figure it out was to spend more time with each candidate and dig into their backgrounds a bit more. I scheduled another round of interviews, this time to get to know each of them better. I forced myself to be completely present and listen to every word said. I dug into seemingly benign statements and pulled at every thread I could, challenging myself to set aside biases. I brought two other teammates along who I knew were independent thinkers and would challenge my assumptions. In the end, we all agreed that my initial gut feeling was right. There was something off with the woman I hadn't connected with. And the woman I was rooting for—I saw that she wasn't right for the role either, at least not yet. I chose to mentor her instead and help her find a better career path. Since none of the candidates were the right fit, we restructured the role and filled it internally, and we all felt good about our collective decision in the end.

But I wouldn't have made the right decision if I hadn't questioned my thinking and examined where my biases were coming from. Going with the team's first pick would have been a mistake, and so would choosing the underdog candidate.

Put It into Practice: How to Question Your Thoughts

You can ask yourself some questions when you feel passionate (okay, defensive) about how you think or feel or when you are judgmental about a person or a situation. I have found that at times, I can detach from my thoughts, and sometimes I can't, but this process always helps me put things into perspective. By asking yourself these kinds of questions, you may find that you will be more open, compassionate, and tolerant of others, leading to contentment.

- Why do I believe this? Why are my feelings so strong?
- What if I believed something different? What would change?
- What story am I telling myself about this person or situation? How do I know that story is true? What other stories could also be true?
- What assumptions am I making?

- What would happen if I just let this thought/feeling go, and it never crossed my mind again? Will anything change?
- Is this how I really feel, or is my ego getting in the way?
- Why am I being judgmental?
- What if these thoughts are the truth? Would I do something different?

• • •

Most of us can agree that the world would be a better place if we weren't always arguing, judging, defending, and warring. If we want to change this about our world, we must change ourselves first, committing to a more open-minded approach. You can start by being more curious about your thoughts and pausing to consider that belief doesn't necessarily equate to truth and that it's okay, even beneficial, that your truth isn't everyone else's truth.

14

USE SELF-DISCIPLINE FOR SUCCESS

Self-discipline is a highly critical attribute to becoming successful. It's almost impossible to achieve excellence without it. Self-discipline helps you stay focused on what needs to be done to reach your goals; it gives you the grit to stick with it, even when something is difficult. It helps you choose to win the long game over short-term gratification. Self-discipline allows you to overcome obstacles and deal with the discomfort of pushing yourself to new heights.

What exactly is self-discipline? It's essentially the ability to control your impulses, emotions, reactions, and behaviors. It is taking ownership of your commitments to yourself and others and following through when you make promises. It's the ability to forego short-term gratification in favor of long-term satisfaction and gain. It's saying no when you really want to say yes.

I developed self-discipline as a result of being a collegiate athlete. I had to work out, practice, rest, eat well, and be mentally tough to perform at my best. And since I attended the Colorado School of Mines, I also had to keep up with my studies, as my coach had little tolerance for poor grades. To balance it all, I had to stay disciplined. I found that to-do lists helped me stay focused, prioritizing my homework by difficulty and test schedule allowed me to get decent grades, cooking for myself kept me healthy, working out first thing in the morning was the only way I got it done, and showing up at practice prepared to work hard made me a better teammate. Taking a break from being disciplined helped, too. I didn't beat myself up if I got off track; instead, I simply picked up where I left off and started the cycle again.

I carried this discipline into my professional life, too, despite my substance abuse issues. I always prioritized work, no matter how hungover I was. Today, I get up before 5:00 a.m. to work out and prepare for my day. I use a scorecard with my CEO coach to ensure that I am working on long-term, strategic initiatives rather than being lulled into the complacency that putting out daily fires brings. Discipline matters.

Speaking of coaches, you already know I am a huge believer in how much value they add as accountability buddies. After threatening to write a book for years, I finally hired a writing coach and joined a writing cohort. The thought of showing up to our biweekly meetings without hitting my goal of 5,000 written words was just what I needed to get the book done.

Being self-disciplined isn't about leading a restrictive and boring life void of enjoyment, relaxation, and fun. In fact, it's next to impossible to be self-disciplined in all areas of your life, and I don't recommend it. Instead, it helps to use self-discipline to focus your energies on what's most important to you. You can use it to help you make the short- and long-term tradeoffs and make better choices.

Put It into Practice:
Create More Self-Discipline

Self-discipline is a learned behavior that will strengthen the more you use it. Start by choosing one thing in your life you want to improve or change and try some of the things I do in my daily life to stay focused and motivated; I call them my self-discipline tricks:

Make a self-discipline list.

You can't achieve your goals without discipline, so supplement your list with what you need to do to be disciplined enough to achieve them. This idea came from the book *The Only Sales Guide You Will Ever Need*, and I love it. It keeps me focused on the behaviors I need to exhibit to reach my goals. For example, one of my goals a few years back was to be more visible to our customers. My discipline list includes "Call three customers per week" and "Send five thank-you cards per month."

Use a daily "to-do" list to track what you need to get done to achieve your goals.

I use Asana to make daily checklists and keep my goal and discipline list here. The software is a great tool to help track, organize, and prioritize things. I make sure that my "to do" list coincides with my discipline list, such as "Call a customer." I love checking the little boxes and watching the unicorn fly away when I've completed a task; it even motivates me to finish one or two more things on my list at the end of the day so that I feel the satisfaction of checking one more box. I've found the best time to create my list for the next day is at the end of my workday, and then I tweak it in the morning before heading to the office.

Figure out what your barriers to success are.

For example, I'm easily distracted by emails, meetings, and people walking into my office. To reach my goal of more customer contact, I close my office door as soon as I get to work and make calls, send thank-you notes, and answer emails sent from customers. I then check it off my list and move on with my day.

Are you trying to lose weight? Get the junk food out of your house. Want to be more productive at work? Close your email application and only check your emails twice per day. If you want to get in shape, get up early and work out so you don't lose motivation when you are tired at the end of the day. Minimize or remove all temptations and distractions to reach your most important goals.

Share your goals with others.

It's easier to stick with something when you've made a public commitment; the thought of failing in front of others can motivate you to stick with it. These people can help hold you accountable, too. Invite someone to be your accountability buddy and ask them to tell you when they see you veering off course.

Do it for someone else.

I know the saying goes, "Don't do it for others; do it for yourself," but I have found I am much more disciplined when considering how my actions, behaviors, emotions, and impulses affect others. Contrary to popular belief, it's okay to use external sources to drive motivation. In fact, sometimes, external motivators are more powerful than internal ones.

Create or break habits.

You create discipline through creating habits. Once something becomes a habit, you no longer need the willpower to force yourself to behave a certain way. For example, one of my recent goals was to do more yoga, as it makes me feel stronger and clear-headed. I started by committing to doing yoga thirty minutes every day for thirty days. I saw such benefits that I stuck with it after the thirty days. Now I get up an hour earlier in the morning to start my day off with sixty minutes of yoga. I don't even have to set the alarm anymore. I highly recommend reading *The Power of Habit* by Charles Duhigg. The book will give you all kinds of insight.

Stop making excuses.

Don't wait for tomorrow; do it now. Fall off the wagon? Start over immediately. Quit telling yourself something is too hard or that you can't change. Don't blame other people for your circumstances. Excuse-making is the killer of self-discipline; it allows you to let yourself off the hook. You can achieve so much more in life if you adopt the Nike mindset: *just do it*.

• • •

You are the master of your destiny, the creator of your life. If you want your future to look and feel a certain way, you must develop the discipline to get there. While it seems counter-intuitive, I have found that I am happier and healthier the more self-disciplined I become. I think you will find the same thing, too.

Sure, I am busy, and I work hard. I still make tradeoffs, and there are times when I must put work in front of my family. But my life is relatively balanced, and I only say yes to the things that are *most* important to me. I am happier and more satisfied than I've ever been in my life.

I am not alone. Weebly CFO Kim Jabal says that the key to work-life integration is a flexible schedule, both at work and at home. "The only way that anyone can balance work and family or work and personal life is if everyone within an organization agrees that 'life balance' is critical to the overall well-being of employees and the productivity and effectiveness of the company," Jabal told *Business Insider* during a recent interview. She describes her plan, "Home an hour in the morning, get kids to school, work in the office 9:00 a.m. to 5:00 p.m., have dinner with kids, work three hours at night."

And I've gotten really good at saying no. You can, too.

Put It into Practice: Create More Balance

Prioritize your life.

Make a list of the essential things in your life—the things that you absolutely cannot give up (i.e., family, work, health). Then make a list of what you want your future to look like. I can promise you this—to be the future version of yourself, you must have intention *and* take action. If you are too busy to work on the future version of yourself, it will be hard to get there.

Next, make a list of all the other things you do that aren't vitally important to your life and all the things you do that don't help you get to the future version of you. Next to each of those, list a few ways you can shed them from your life. Then pick two or three and reduce or eliminate them. It really can be that easy.

Just say no.

I was worried that people would judge me for not giving back more when I stopped doing so much. Instead, whenever I said no and explained why, I received a reply like this: "I wish I would have done that more often." It's okay to say no, and if you want balance in life, you must do it more often. And remember, "No," is a complete sentence. You don't have to justify protecting your time and well-being.

Take breaks.

Sometimes just a short break is all you need to feel refreshed. Take the afternoon off. Go for a walk on your lunch break. Get a babysitter for an hour and get a massage. Read a novel. Be sure to take breaks throughout your day and week.

Don't overschedule.

Everyone needs time to think and relax, but it's hard to do when your calendar is full. Don't sign your kids up for every activity possible; you'll appreciate it, and they will, too. Avoid back-to-back-to-back meetings. It's okay to block off focus or personal time on your calendar and don't allow others to schedule over it.

Stop trying to be perfect.

Chasing perfectionism is a fruitless effort because it's not attainable. Most times, good enough is good enough, and when you let go of perfectionism, stress levels go down, and you'll feel happier. Remember, the only person who cares about doing something perfectly is you, and the return on perfecting something diminishes quickly once it's good enough, so don't waste precious time.

Move your body every day.

The mood and performance-boosting benefits of working out are irrefutable. Commit to moving your body for at least ten minutes each day. Even better, work up a sweat. Vigorous activities increase endorphins which will make you feel better.

• • •

I love Yahoo CEO Melissa Mayer's advice: "Find your rhythm. Avoiding burnout isn't about getting three square meals or eight hours of sleep. It's not even necessarily about getting time at home," she says. Instead, it's about finding the rhythm. I agree. Balance is not about finding the sweet spot where you can do it all. Rather, it's a give and take where sometimes you give more to work and at other times, you give more to family or your personal life. But if you find your rhythm, you can find more ease in saying no, prioritizing yourself, and letting go of perfection.

16

BE RESILIENT

Being resilient is a must-have trait for a successful CEO who wants to make a big impact. There is nothing easy about running a company, disrupting an industry, developing people, and managing your personal health and well-being. It requires mental toughness and the ability to recover quickly from challenges.

Psychology Today says that resilience "is that ineffable quality that allows some people to be knocked down by life and come back stronger than ever. Rather than letting failure overcome them and drain their resolve, they find a way to rise from the ashes. Psychologists have identified some of the factors that make someone resilient, including a positive attitude, optimism, the ability to regulate emotions, and the ability to see failure as a form of helpful feedback. Even after misfortune, resilient people are blessed with such an outlook that they can change course and soldier on."

Being a strong leader who is driven to achieve isn't always liked or appreciated by everyone. And being the only female sitting on my industry's safety association, I have felt like an outsider, a person who is merely tolerated. I am passionate about improving our industry and spearheaded several initiatives, including a grassroots movement to standardize basic industrial cleaning safety principles worldwide. I worked hard to get the association board to buy in. They agreed to let me take the lead and create a collaborative coalition with other international safety associations to write and promote these standards.

I put a tremendous amount of effort into making this coalition work but, after it picked up steam, was reprimanded by the association's board president. After many conversations, he finally admitted that he didn't care about the initiative and paid very little attention to my quarterly reports. "I didn't think the coalition would go anywhere," he said. "I never really cared about it, and it was my mistake to underestimate you. You are an aggressive person, which has pros and cons. You have a tremendous capability to get things done, and I applaud that. But sometimes, your approach rubs people the wrong way. Sometimes being an overachiever is a bad thing."

He told me repeatedly that his opposition to what I was doing wasn't personal, but I never believed it. StoneAge dominates the industry, but truth be told, anyone could have stepped up and done what we were doing. Our relentless commitment to innovation, safety, and customer service excellence separated us from the rest. And we chose to show up and participate, not to block anyone else from doing so but because we believed in doing our part to advance the industry.

For weeks I struggled with my status on this board: powerful, dominating, successful . . . and disliked. *Should I give up? Should I leave the board? Should I stay on but disengage?* Then one day during a Peloton strength class, the instructor said, "Some people may call you a bitch for your relentless drive to be successful. Stop worrying about it. If someone doesn't like you because you are strong, because you are driven to improve yourself, then fuck them."

I laughed out loud. That was just what I needed to hear. Sure, I don't need to be obnoxious, but I don't need to change my drive to improve the world and make an impact. If people don't like me because I am running a company that's making a difference, so what? At that moment, I decided to let his negative comments go. There is no need to hang on to that baggage; all it would do was weigh me down and make me want to quit the board.

Instead of focusing on my emotions, I focused on finding a solution. A few days later, during a mountain bike ride, an idea popped into my head about creating a win-win, and I resolved the situation where we both got what we wanted.

Leaders must lean into resiliency to find a path forward, bouncing back from setbacks with grace, gratitude, and grit. Here's how.

Put It into Practice: How to Build Resiliency

Take responsibility for everything that happens to you.

The only way you can build resilience is to take responsibility for your life and everything that happens in it. Refuse to play a victim. I don't mean for this to come across as harsh, but if you adopt that mindset that things don't happen *to* you, they happen *because* of you, you will build resiliency. This is the only way to empower yourself to change your situation, no matter what.

Owning it means you can change it. If you want to be resilient, refuse to retreat, deny, ignore, or blame. Remember, things don't happen to you. They happen because of you. And you have the power to create a resilient outcome.

Build your support system.

Having a shoulder to lean on makes all the difference in the world when bouncing back. Resilient people take the time to build a strong network they can rely on to help them through tough times. It doesn't have to be a big network, just a strong one, and one you can depend on to help you when you need it.

If you don't have a strong support system, it's not too late to start. Reach out to a few people you can trust and begin to build friendships. Hire a therapist or a life coach. Lean on members of your family. Don't fall into the trap of telling yourself that you are alone and that no one cares—doing this weakens your "bounce back" muscles.

Stand up for yourself.

It's hard to stand up for yourself. Whether you are afraid of being judged, shunned, laughed at, dismissed, or worse, fired, there are inevitably social and professional risks. But you will never be where you want to be if you don't stand up for yourself.

To me, "standing up for yourself" means asking for what you want, speaking up when you feel you are being mistreated or disrespected, and making tough decisions that maintain boundaries, values, and self-esteem.

Take a deep breath and let it go.

Letting go is the only way to be resilient. There's no point in holding on to negative thoughts and old baggage—all it does is weigh you down. Remember, beating yourself up, not believing in yourself, and letting others squash your confidence decreases your resiliency. So stop the negative self-talk, forgive yourself and anyone else involved, learn from the situation, and move on. Just take a deep breath and let it go. It is what it is; the most important thing is doing what you need to do to move forward.

Don't give up.

Finally, the fastest way to not bounce back is to, well, not bounce back. Giving up is an excuse. Keep trying, keep moving forward. Yes, you will have to change, grow, and ask for feedback. Perhaps you will have to get professional help. But whatever you do, don't give up—not if you want a happy and successful life. Think of the most successful people you know. Maybe they seem like they just breeze through life, but in reality, they, too, have had to overcome setbacks and negative experiences. You must dig deep and summon the determination to handle whatever life throws at you and to persevere no matter what.

Practice gratitude.

As my friend Chris Schembra says in his book, *Gratitude Through Hard Times: Finding Positive Benefits Through Our Darkest Hours*, "I personally think resiliency is sexy. I'd rather be complimented on my resilience through adversity than on some unique talent or physical trait." I agree; I am most proud of my resiliency in the face of every challenge I've faced. I am deeply grateful for my struggles; if it weren't for my overdose, I wouldn't be where I am today. You, too, can find the gift in the hard things. Follow Chris's advice and journal about five of your character traits that allowed you to be resilient in the face of adversity. And then give gratitude for your journey for its resiliency that determines success.

• • •

I think back to that day I was lying on the floor of my apartment, willing myself to live even though I was questioning if I actually wanted to. It was the lowest point of my life. I was filled with shame, dread, and fear. I had no money and a big drug problem. I am where I am today because I did not give up on myself that day. I worked hard to rebuild my life. I proved to myself that I could bounce back from anything.

Life takes all kinds of twists and turns. Sometimes it meanders along; other times, it feels like everything is right on track. Then again, maybe sometimes it feels like it's in free-fall toward rock bottom. Being resilient allows you to go with the flow, no matter the situation. Don't let your mistakes and failures take you down. Look at them as research on how not to do something and bounce back stronger than before.

If there is anything that I hope to leave with you it is the courage to take action, whether it's one small step or embarking on a significant life transition. You can create a better life. You can bounce back from hard things. You are resilient.

PART THREE
LEADING OTHERS

appreciated his experience and history in the industry. He gave me good advice and encouraged me to build relationships with our customers, suppliers, and everyone in the company. "Hard work will only get you so far," he said. "To build an exceptional company, what matters is the quality of your relationships." Our meetings helped me gain confidence in my decision-making, and I learned how to talk through various scenarios and plan for potential outcomes. He enjoyed mentoring me and we grew closer and continue to do so today. There is no better way to build a strong relationship than by spending time together, hearing each other out and strategizing over the company's future.

I took his advice to heart, and I carried it with me over the next decade as I developed open, transparent, and trust-based relationships with John and his cofounder Jerry. I asked their opinions, took advice, communicated regularly, and made them feel part of the team. I looked forward to their mentorship and ensured they were in the loop.

Looking back, I understand that the outcome could have been very different. And I know now how often founders and hired guns butt heads. It's hard for founders to give up control and let professional management change the organization, and it's difficult for hired CEOs to listen to advice and direction given by founders. Both parties want to do it their way.

It's difficult to guess whether or not another CEO would have successfully taken over for John and Jerry, but I believe it would have been much harder if the company had selected someone else for the role. Because I showed up with humility and curiosity and truly cared about learning from them, it made it easier for them to let go and hand the reigns to me. I never went to battle with them; instead, I took the approach of finding a mutually agreeable solution.

I have a tremendous amount of respect for these two men. They took a risk on me. They also knew they had to give me some autonomy to see if I had what it took to successfully lead their company. Looking back, I believe there were a few things we did well to make it a successful transition.

Put It into Practice: How to Transition Well

Create a transition plan.

First, John and Jerry laid out a transition plan, giving me a few years to gain experience. I took on more responsibilities as I learned about the industry and organization and earned their trust and respect. We identified goals and discussed milestones in advance, and they set clear expectations for me. I also learned how to communicate my needs and expectations from them. We developed a two-way communication street that included guidance, feedback, education, and status reporting.

If you're facilitating or involved in a high-level transition in your organization, take the initiative early on to scope out the process and define small steps toward completion. Having a clear plan will reduce confusion and the chance of power struggles. Everyone does better when they understand expectations, which is especially important in a transition of executive leadership.

Study company history.

Additionally, I worked hard to understand the company's history and John and Jerry's decision-making philosophy to figure out how to build upon it rather than change it. While the culture morphed as I grew in my leadership capabilities, I believe the transition was successful because I showed a healthy respect for what they created and learned how to fit with their styles rather than forcing them to adapt to my way of doing things.

As you transition into executive leadership, don't underestimate the power of history. Understand the company's history not only from the founder's perspective but from long-term employees and customers. Be knowledgeable about the company's values and business philosophy and respect its roots and culture. No one wants to work for a leader who doesn't value the work that's been put into the company to get it where it is today, even if it's struggling.

Develop healthy relationships.

John, Jerry, and I also developed healthy relationships with each other. I was honest and direct, as were they. I asked their opinions and always credited them for building such a unique and caring company. I was transparent in all my decisions, and I owned my mistakes. They gave me constructive feedback and praised my efforts and successes. The three of us developed trust quickly, making it easy to talk about growing the company, building the team, and taking over their legacy. Most importantly, I knew they had my back, making it safe to try new things to scale the company and take some risks.

Don't be afraid to take feedback and advice from previous leadership. So often, we feel the need to prove ourselves and that the only way to do that is to push aside others to make room for yourself. That almost never works. Instead, commit to doing your part to build healthy relationships with those you are taking over for. Be curious and spend time getting to know them. Don't be afraid to question things and push back, just do so respectfully. Use your transition plan to navigate conflict or disagreement.

Respect new roles and responsibilities.

Finally, the transition was successful because John and Jerry gave me the authority to do my job. They rarely undermined me, and when it did happen, the undermining was unintentional, and we worked through it collaboratively without getting defensive. John and Jerry didn't meddle in the day-to-day and gave me enough rope to chart my path; in fact, they let me be me, which I greatly appreciate. They continue to be involved with the company—John as the board chairman and Jerry as a product engineer, which allows them to stay connected to the company they spent decades growing. I believe their involvement creates a competitive advantage for us. They help us stay grounded in our reason for being: to take care of our employees and customers. Their involvement keeps the board focused on creating meaningful, well-paying jobs that create real value for our employees. Their vision to be an employee-owned company builds the value of our ESOP, allowing our employees—the ones creating value for our customers—to share in the company's success.

• • •

If you've laid the foundation with a clear transition plan and you've taken time to build relationships, it's easier to respect roles and responsibilities—but it still takes effort. When lines start to blur, which they eventually will, you must approach it with a level head. Getting angry or letting things fester won't create a smooth transition. Talk about roles and responsibilities frequently and address the overlap rationally and with an intent to resolve issues positively. Not all founders and exiting executives are so willing to give up control, but wrestling it away from them will cause more resistance and may lead to a failed transition.

I buy into John and Jerry's legacy, and I am honored not just to be part of it but to make it more substantial. Our shared vision, commitment, and trust made it a successful transition.

18

MAKE BOLD MOVES

Astronaut Chris Hadfield said, "Almost everything worthwhile carries with it some sort of risk, whether it's starting a new business, whether it's leaving home, whether it's getting married, or whether it's flying in space." In life and leadership, we are always pivoting, always disrupting ourselves.

A common trait of most CEOs is that they take a risk or make a bold move that sets the CEO's trajectory. According to the CEO Genome Project, a study by Elena L Botelho and Kim R. Powell, 45 percent of CEO candidates have had a career blowup. More than half of CEOs took a smaller role at some point in their career to build something from scratch or make a bigger impact. Over 30 percent of CEOs made a big leap in their careers, taking a risk to try something new or a role outside of their expertise.*

This is exactly what I did in 2006 when I picked my broken life and unhealthy body off the floor of my apartment in Austin and followed

---

* Elena Lytkina et. al., "The Fastest Path to the CEO Job, according to a 10-Year Study," *Harvard Business Review*, January 31, 2018, https://hbr.org/2018/01/the-fastest-path-to-the-ceo-job-according-to-a-10-year-study.

my heart to Durango. Maybe even if I didn't make this big move I'd still be a CEO today, but deep in my heart, I doubt it. I left a high-paying sales job to start over in a small town where good jobs are hard to come by. And I am proud of where I am now. Bold moves opened the possibility of living a bold life.

When you become a CEO, taking smart risks and pivoting are critical to success. And if you want to disrupt your industry, there is no way around it—you have to make bold moves.

The first bold move I made as a CEO was to completely upend our business model. As our products became more complex and technical, it was clear that our sales model, selling through distributors, was holding us back. Our products were improving and changing rapidly, and the people selling them to our customers were not experts in their operation; it just wasn't effective any longer. In the fall of 2015, we decided to sell directly to our customers in North America and dramatically reduce our dependence on distributors. We followed suit in Europe in 2017. Our decision infuriated our dealers, but I was confident it was the right decision. We opened five locations in two years, started a rental business, and developed deep relationships with our customers, which has paid off in numerous ways.

One of the hardest things to do is deliver bad news. I'll never forget flying across the country in October 2015, personally meeting with every dealer to deliver the news; I traveled to six states in two days. I can't imagine that there is anyone out there who would enjoy this responsibility, but doing so was an important part of my journey and our transition into a bold new business model. I was putting the future of StoneAge first, but my mantra "compassion, grace, and gratitude" was always top of mind. That's how I wanted to deliver my message, always keeping in mind the importance of treating my fellow human beings with dignity and respect, and always being grateful for the experience and the relationships—even when it's uncomfortable and even as I upset many people because of my decisions.

Our next bold move involved a major pivot in technology. For quite a while, I had known that I wanted to increase StoneAge's capabilities and enter the technology space, specifically software and data.

The concept of the Internet of Things (IoT) was new to me, and I knew very little about the intricacies of the industry. *Oxford Dictionary* describes IoT as "the interconnection via the internet of computing devices embedded in everyday objects, enabling them to send and receive data." Or more simply put—smart products.

I spent a significant amount of time reading articles on IoT, reading about various consulting business models, and learning about our competition. I was curious about how other companies performing product development services scaled. I wondered how we could differentiate ourselves in such a fragmented but growing space. These questions compelled me to learn more, and soon, I had a clear picture of what we needed to do to take the company to the next level: I wanted to acquire StoneAge's IoT product development partner, Breadware.

At the time of closing, we were in the beginning stages of the pandemic, and it was a risky move. I asked myself questions like *Should I spend cash on this acquisition or conserve cash to see how the economic shutdown plays out?* I spent countless nights wondering if I was making the right call. In the end, I trusted my instincts. Based on our due diligence, I knew the company was healthy enough and could absorb the hit if our projections didn't play out. The company's vision was crystal clear, and there was no doubt that the acquisition fit strategically.

Once the acquisition was finalized, the hard work of integration and learning the industry began. At first, it was a bit overwhelming as I didn't have in-depth knowledge of electronic component design, so I started with my usual "ask a lot of questions and learn" mindset.

We reorganized the team, developed a strategy, built a new website, and executed our plan. And it paid off. In a few short months, the company was outperforming against our KPIs. This bold move was a good move, even though hindsight is always 20/20. Even better, the acquisition of Breadware would positively impact StoneAge in more ways than one. Not only would they be able to help us develop IoT-enabled products faster, but they would help us diversify and put us closer to achieving our vision of transforming from a traditional manufacturing company to a "Solutions as a Service" tech company.

According to a study done by Michael Birshan, a senior partner at McKinsey & Company, when CEOs who take over lagging companies make "bold, decisive moves and adopt an outsider's perspective when they evaluate the business, whether they themselves come from within or outside the company," they improve company performance up to 4.3 percent more than their peers who don't make bold moves. This isn't trivial. Leaders who can look around the corner to see what's coming and position their companies to take advantage by being strategic and decisive and taking some risks have a better chance of being highly successful than those who stay complacent.

Fear of short-term pain is real, and many CEOs don't dare to take the risk. Take Bill George, for example. In his first year as CEO of Medtronic—a medical device company—he decided against acquiring a fast-growing but potentially risky angioplasty company. While those risks were real, they were facing patent issues and pricing pressure; their competitor Boston Scientific bought the company instead. This acquisition, combined with Boston Scientific's market positioning, catapulted innovation and created a sizeable competitor for Medtronic. Bill George said of the acquisition, "I didn't have the courage to accept short-term risk to create a long-term gain. It took Medtronic two decades of expensive research and development programs and additional acquisitions to become the leader in this field."

I truly believe it takes bold moves to build an exceptional company. Blending courage, instinct, and data with a focused plan and hard work are key to ensuring that the moves pay off.

Put It into Practice: How to Make Bold Moves

Be clear on your vision.

If you want to make bold moves that have a higher likelihood of success, make sure your vision is clear and that it stays relevant. As technology and expectations change, industries are expected to improve and adjust accordingly to serve customers well. When your vision is clear, you can understand how potential bold moves can fit into your strategy. StoneAge's vision is to lead the industrial cleaning industry in robotic cleaning solutions. If this wasn't crystal clear, we wouldn't have seen how impactful our the Breadware acquisition would be to our longevity and success.

Do your research.

Understanding what lies ahead will help you feel more comfortable making bold moves. Relying only on gut instinct and intuition while making big decisions will not lead to sustained success. Take the time to research and understand the pros and cons, benefits, and tradeoffs. Talk to experts in the industry or field where you want to make your bold move, get the inside scoop, and read industry publications.

Create a plan.

Big moves aren't always considered *bold* moves. Bold moves are considered as such when the risk-taker reaches success after calculating risk and weighing probable outcomes. Big moves—to put it simply—are risky moves taken with little forethought, which are considered foolish, ill-advised, or shortsighted and often end in failure. To increase your chance of success, develop a robust plan around integration and implementation. A well-thought-out plan will allow you to evaluate opportunities and adjust or pivot when necessary. It should include your go-to-market strategy, deliverables and outcomes, integration activities, and resource identification and allocation.

Do the work.

Bold moves will almost always require hard work. The good news is that if you have a well-thought-out plan, the work effort should be clearly defined and executable. Stay focused and do the work. For example, after buying Breadware, I went to Reno, Nevada, for six weeks to evaluate the team, create a robust plan, restructure the company, and meet clients. Could I have done all of this without immersing myself in the company? Sure, but it would have taken a lot longer to turn them around, build relationships, and see a positive ROI on the acquisition. I was willing to do the work, leading to a winning outcome and a positive, bold move—and I had a strong team back at headquarters, ready to support the effort. Not that there weren't trade-offs to be made. It was the summer of 2020, and the world was in disarray due to the COVID-19 pandemic. StoneAge saw a significant drop in sales that summer, and during my stay in Reno, we went through a 5 percent reduction in workforce. My team in Durango had to pick up the slack and lead the layoffs. It was a very difficult time for all of us, and I felt guilty not being at headquarters to calm the collective nerves of the company. But we managed it well, and it was an excellent opportunity for my executive team to step up and exhibit the ownership mindset. They did an exceptional job leading the company while I focused on Breadware.

Give it time.

It takes time to see your hard work and vision come together. To repeat what Jeff Bezos said, "Planting seeds that will grow into meaningful new businesses takes some discipline, a bit of patience and a nurturing culture." In my experience, it takes a few years to see the real results of a bold move. For a person like me, and I can imagine for you, too, it takes discipline to remain patient. We all want fast results because it shows that our bold move was the right move. It proves that you successfully pulled it off. But bold moves rarely work that way. Sometimes you take a step backward to leapfrog forward. Sometimes it simply takes longer than you think or want. To help with this, I remind myself that evolution is a slow process and there is no such thing as overnight success. It takes disciplined, consistent effort to build an empire. And I would way rather build a lasting empire than be a one-hit wonder.

• • •

Don't be afraid to make well-calculated bold moves. You'll gain valuable experiences, even if they don't work out the way you think. Plus, every time you get out of your comfort zone, you'll expand your competency zone and gain confidence in your ability to disrupt yourself lead your team and company to new heights.

19

KNOW WHERE
YOU ARE GOING

The idea of strategy is simple. It's the combination of your vision, your decision-making process, and a plan of action to achieve that vision. In *Good Strategy/Bad Strategy: The Difference and Why It Matters*, Richard Rumelt said, "A leader's most important job is creating and constantly adjusting this strategic bridge between goals and objectives." Even though it's simple, developing and executing a strategy is hard.

I have learned a great deal about winning strategies, losing strategies, and taking on too much as an organization. I love ideas and trying new things; when the opportunities in front of you are endless, this combination can be dangerous. I have learned this lesson the hard way—repeatedly. Having been accused of liking shiny objects, a label I despise, I have finally figured out the value of focus.

When I came to StoneAge, the strategy was simple yet effective: Build high-quality waterjetting tools for every hydroblasting application at a fair price; work with a strong dealer network to reduce competition;

and grow market share internationally. I connected with this strategy successfully during my first years as CEO, growing the company by double digits each year except for 2008, when we effectively remained flat while many of our competitors crashed. Still, I could see that the desire for automation and robotics would disrupt our industry. These technological advancements would make our customers' work easier, safer, and more efficient. To stay relevant, we would have to modify our product offering, which would bring a slew of changes to our organization.

At the end of 2013 and my fourth year as CEO, we decided to broaden our product offerings and develop automated equipment for industrial cleaning applications. I immediately got myself into trouble. Why? Because I tried to use the old strategy—meant for our traditional business—with a much more complex and service-intensive product line. Being a new and young CEO, I didn't really "get" strategy. I didn't know how to analyze business models, nor did I understand the ramifications of having a "shoot from the hip" methodology to planning. I equated strategy with ideas, ambition, and visionary leadership, but there is a lot more to it than that. At the time, I had no idea how to formulate an effective, cohesive strategy that blends ambition with thoughtful decision-making.

My journey is one to learn from. While in the end, we were successful, we made so many mistakes along the way—mistakes that cost us time and money and put our reputation at risk. Our culture took a hit as people worked hard but felt as if they were spinning their wheels.

The first mistake I made was trying to force-fit a completely different type of product into our existing product strategy philosophy. When you are developing something that your industry hasn't seen before, it requires a comprehensive market fit and go-to-market plan. We didn't do that. I assumed that if we did what we had always done, we would be equally as successful. What made StoneAge successful was that we had similarly functioning tools for a wide variety of applications. We took the same approach with automated equipment and set out to develop a product for every application. This was ambitious, expensive, and wasteful. With small, handheld tools, the only way to scale was to have a tool for every application. But we learned that the process of designing, launching, and selling electromechanical products is far more complex than what's required to develop handheld, manually operated tools. With extensive, complex automation, focusing on one application would have been a much more successful strategy.

Being a small company in rural Colorado, it made sense that we used distributors to sell our products throughout the world. We spent decades building a robust dealer network that we relied heavily on to help us grow. As we developed automated equipment, I assumed our dealers would be excited to sell more expensive product lines and we pushed them to actively sell our new equipment. Believing that our dealer network could sell this more complex equipment was my second mistake. This was not the case. The sales cycle was long and the investment in demo equipment and inventory high, two things a dealer network doesn't like, especially if they are not equipped for this type of product. Having a middleman between you and your customers when you develop products that have never been seen wreaked havoc on our engineering team. It was impossible to get clear product requirements and iterative design testing partners when your dealers try to keep you away from the people using your tools.

The third mistake I made was underestimating the amount of field support this type of equipment would require. Trying to service products out of Durango, Colorado, is a travel nightmare, especially when your closest customer is in the Gulf Coast of Texas and your furthest one is in Australia or Singapore. This was exacerbated by the fact that I had assumed our dealer network could handle the service aspect, which many couldn't. To be frank, very few in our industry were equipped to support the changes we were driving through our innovative product development.

The underlying issue was that we didn't do enough market research and product development planning, which caused us to underestimate the seismic changes we were leading our industry toward. It wasn't neglect that caused these missteps; we move fast as a company, and my inexperience in leading this kind of change bit me. I didn't ask enough questions, and my ambition to disrupt our industry stifled the voice in the back of my head that said, *Maybe we should slow down!*

These mistakes led to more mistakes as we changed our business model, sales model, and product development processes. We tried to fix all our problems at once while also pursuing a multitude of opportunities that came our way, which spread the team too thin and begged the question: *Where are we going, and can we actually get all this work done?*

One evening in 2018, I was watching *Alice in Wonderland* with my son Jack, and I was struck by the conversation between Alice and the Cheshire Cat, which sums up the importance of having a vision and a plan.

"Would you tell me, please, which way I ought to go from here?" asked Alice.

"That depends a good deal on where you want to get to," said the Cat.

"I don't much care where—" said Alice.

"Then it doesn't matter which way you go," said the Cat.

"—so long as I get SOMEWHERE," Alice added as an explanation.

"Oh, you're sure to do that," said the Cat, "if you only walk long enough."

I sat back on the couch, stunned. *Oh my god!* I thought. *This is me! I am traveling on fifteen different paths, trying to achieve our vision of becoming the leader in industrial cleaning automation and robotics. And by trying to do it all, I am risking our reputation for being a successful, well-respected company that solves its customers' problems and is a great place to work.*

Luckily, through our employee-owners' brute force effort and commitment, we were able to execute a poorly articulated strategy. No matter the workload, the team rallied behind our many goals, and we pulled off what many companies can't: a complete change in business model with a crappy plan while maintaining our culture of being a great place to work. But we could've avoided many challenges, setbacks, and frustrations if we'd been more focused and intentional in our strategizing.

Put It into Practice: How to Build a Winning Strategy

There are many ways to develop a strategy. I am not saying our way is the right way, but here is how we do it—and I know this works.

Create a vision of where you want to go.

Having a vision is foundational to creating success. A clear, well-articulated vision gives you direction and a larger purpose. It gives you the inspiration to work hard and be disciplined. Once you establish your vision, it allows you to define success and set proper expectations for what you want to accomplish. Remember, you can't get to where you want to go if you don't know where you are going!

To create a vision, consider what your organization's goal is and what it will look like once you accomplish it. This vision could illustrate a financial milestone, employee engagement improvements, product or service advancements, or a combination of all of them. Knowing exactly what it is you're after provides you with the guidance needed to step closer to it through action. I found it helpful to imagine what our industry was going to look like in ten years and then strategize about how we would not just meet the industry's needs but embed us in their processes. In fact, I drafted a ten-year vision that I adjust every year as we march towards our vision and learn new things or acquire new companies.

Describe the problem you are trying to solve.

As Richard Rumelt writes in *Good Strategy/Bad Strategy*, "The core of strategy work is always the same: discovering the critical factors in a situation and designing a way of coordinating and focusing actions on dealing with those factors." You must be able to diagnose the situation before you can formulate a plan. The first page of our strategy deck consists of these two things: our vision and the problem we are trying to solve in two sentences or less.

When you are developing the strategy to achieve your vision, ask yourself: *What problem am I trying to solve?* This is the essence of strategy, although many leaders don't articulate it this way. You should always develop your strategy around your vision and the problem you are trying to solve for your customers or organization on your way to achieving your vision. It's hard to distill a vision and problem statement into a few sentences, but trust me, it's worth it to force yourself to do it. It's the only way to create a simple plan that everyone in your organization can understand and feel part of.

Break down your vision into segments that are easy to understand.

A high-level vision is the starting point, but you must tie it to people's day-to-day work, and that's why it's important to segment your strategy, so people see how it impacts them. I once had an employee tell me, "Strategy is a management thing. My team does the real work." This is how most people feel about strategy, and it's a problem. Every person on your team needs to understand the strategy and how their work ties to it. If they don't think their work matters in executing the strategy, you aren't doing your job as a leader. We call this "line of sight," which I'll describe later.

Segmentation is the process of dividing a company's business into areas of focus. Customer or product segmentation is common, but you can also use segmentations to organize your strategy and you can segment it in many ways. For example, you could segment by business unit, department, or strategic initiatives. At StoneAge, we have four overarching segments in which we look at our work, all tied to the StoneAge Assurance Promise: products and services, customer service excellence, business optimization, and culture. We break down the specifics of our vision for each segment, so it's clear how each one helps us achieve the overall vision. This allows our functional leaders understand their role in strategy execution and create initiatives and operational plans that align with the vision, focusing their teams' activities on work that moves the company toward the vision. Without specifics, all you have is a vision on a piece of paper.

Create initiatives for each segment.

I hate annual planning meetings and think they are a waste of time. A strategy is always evolving, and there is no end game. That's why we plan our strategy real-time and assess quarterly. We set major initiatives for each segment; some might be short initiatives, and some might be multi-year initiatives. The executive team reviews our progress bi-weekly and adjusts our plan as we go. As you build your initiatives, be specific and tie it to the problem you are trying to solve. For example, we are expanding our service offerings as part of our vision. Our initiatives sound something like this:

- Research, analyze, and select a learning management system.
- Craft ten new courses to populate learning management system.
- Integrate and implement learning management system.
- Launch new training program.

Create departmental and cross-departmental goals for each initiative.

This is how you create a "line of sight." Every person in the organization should be able to see how the work they do impacts the strategy. Keep track of these goals in a project management system such as Asana or Trello, so there are accountability and visibility.

In the example just discussed, we would set specific goals, timelines, and outcomes for each bullet point and assign them an owner.

Executive management commitments.

Every major initiative should have an executive-level sponsor. Bi-weekly, each sponsor updates the executive team on the progress and goals for the next bi-weekly meeting. All issues should be on the table, including roadblocks, constraints, mistakes, and communication breakdowns. The team should also celebrate wins and agree on recognizing a job well done throughout the organization. This creates accountability and ensures that the right conversations are being had at the executive management level. This takes trust, commitment, and open, candid dialog. But if done right, you can quickly solve problems and adjust before an initiative gets off track.

Annual planning should be done more than annually.

Despite my feelings on annual planning, we do have a one-day annual planning session, but it's more of a team-building activity than a full-blown, sit at a whiteboard and plan kind of session. We talk about the big picture and debate what we got right during the year and what we got wrong and determine what tweaks need to be made the following year. You certainly shouldn't be reinventing the plan every year. There is nothing more unsettling to an organization to feel like the company is going in a new direction every year. I know from experience because my employees felt this way in those years of poor strategy design.

• • •

Many leaders confuse operational leadership with strategic leadership. If you follow this process for creating a winning strategy, you won't make this mistake.

20

BUILD A TEAM

A few years ago, I was having a conversation with Howard M. Shore, executive coach and CEO of the Activate Group, on my podcast, *Reflect Forward*, and he said, "the most important skill a leader must have is the ability to build a team." It was a striking statement: simple, accurate, and hard to do.

If you want to be successful, put most of your effort toward building a great team. Most leaders don't realize this, and it took me many years and many hiring mistakes to recognize this necessity. Some of my missteps were partly because of my immaturity as a leader. I mistakenly thought I needed to be the glue that held the team together. And because I excelled at navigating hard conversations, individual team members would come to me to complain about each other. I would then step in to help solve the problem. But all it did was make things worse. Instead of teaching people how to navigate the issues they had with each other, I would triangulate for them and try to be the intermediary. When I would bring a new person onto the team, the pattern would repeat, and it would be difficult for the new hire to integrate into the team. I didn't realize that by trying to fix all the problems, I was creating a toxic environment that didn't promote teamwork and personal development. Even worse, my team relied on me to solve interpersonal problems, and I became a counselor to a few of them.

So, you can imagine how important it was for me to learn how to build a strong team.

What defines a great team? Simply put, it's cohesion. If you do not have a cohesive team, it's hard to be a high-performing company. *Merriam-Webster* defines cohesion as "the act or state of sticking together tightly." When applied to a team, I describe it as each team member working in tandem for the good of the whole. What makes a cohesive team? Trust, communication, collective belief in the mission, and being a giver rather than a taker.

Trust

Trust is the foundation in any successful relationship, and creating a high-performing team is imperative. Each member must trust each other to show up with a positive mindset, work hard, and keep it real. To build trust, every person must care about building relationships. To build a relationship, you must be honest, do what you say you will do, own your mistakes, and genuinely care about the person as a colleague. Without trust, a team will fail.

Communication

I believe that most of the problems we face today result from communication breakdowns. When a team communicates well, exceptions are clear, change is managed, people feel heard, issues are solved efficiently,

Develop Team Operating Principles

In their book, *The CEO Test: Master the Challenges That Make or Break Leaders,* authors Adam Bryant and Kevin Sharer outline the need for team operating principles. They say, "Building, managing, and developing a team can seem like a full-time job on its own, but the investment of time will pay significant dividends for leaders if they answer these foundational questions to ensure the team is operating at its highest possible level: What is our purpose? Do we have the best people on the team? Are we clear on how we are going to work together? Am I, as the leader, owning the responsibilities of running the team and personally coaching everyone to get better?"

I spent years formulating our executive team operating principles as I learned how to lead and build teams. I am still surprised at how long it took for us to get them right. Now, we live and breathe our operating principles, and we regularly check in on where we are succeeding and where we are falling short.

I've included the StoneAge executive management team's operating principles in the Appendix on page 277. I highly recommend you lead your team through the exercise of developing your own version, then weave them into your meetings and performance reviews. We survey ourselves quarterly and adjust as necessary. And the best part? My team holds themselves and each other accountable for each of these points.

Why? Because they developed them based on their own frustration with peers who didn't show up the way we needed them to. Because they see the benefit of being part of and contributing to a healthy, high-performing team.

Avoid Hiring Mistakes

Hiring is hard, and no matter how good your process is, it is still a crapshoot. It takes time to get to know people, and it's impossible to vet all of the nuances in the interview process. We used a modified version of "The Who Method for Hiring," a simple four-step process for hiring outlined in a book by Geoff Smart and Randy Street.* Using the "Who" process improved our success rate dramatically. But we still get it wrong some of the time.

To the detriment of the team and company, I have made the mistake of hiring experience over culture. Some schools of thought believe you shouldn't hire for cultural fit, but I disagree. Understanding your culture and what it takes to succeed in it matters greatly. At StoneAge, we care as much about your teamwork, mindset, and belief in the mission as we do about the quality and quantity of your work.

When you are a small but growing company, it's tempting to bring in senior leaders who have worked in larger companies, thinking they can help you scale. Giving in to this temptation a few times, I have let smart, talented executives go less than a year into the job because they could not do the job, both from an effort and a team cohesion perspective. Hiring and firing leadership is disruptive to the organization, and it causes the people you fire to dislike you.

The StoneAge culture is very much a cross-departmental collaboration and "roll up your sleeves" to get the job done, no matter your position in the company. We are very much like a startup—a forty-year-old startup. Sitting in your office directing your managers and getting upset when your peers get in your lane doesn't work for us. But in many cases, this is what high-level managers do at big companies. I have found that the pace, collaboration, team cohesion requirements, and type of work are

---

* Geoff Smart and Randy Street, *Who: The A Method for Hiring* (New York: Ballantine Books, 2008).

BUILD A TEAM   175

not what they are used to, nor what they are looking for, no matter what is said in the interview.

Don't compromise your team and company values for the sake of experience. Always hire for fit, teamwork, and character. You can teach people skills, but you can't teach humility, character, and integrity.

Put It into Practice: Ways to Build a Stronger Team

In developing my own team-building skills and helping others do the same, I have found that accomplishing these six things will help a good manager become a *great* manager.

Connect through regular one-on-one meetings.

The best way to build strong relationships is to have regular one-on-one meetings with each team member. Most people want to share certain aspects of their lives and appreciate when their boss takes the time to get to know them better, especially regarding personal and career aspirations. Use these one-on-one meetings to ask good questions, discuss professional development and performance, solve problems, and review priorities and projects. Effective one-on-one meetings will result in more effective relationships.

Celebrate the wins and recognize contributions.

There is nothing worse than doing great work and having it go unnoticed or unappreciated. Motivate your employees by recognizing their contributions. Give them a "power thank you." A "power thank you," as defined by Mark Goulston, author and psychologist, has three parts:

1. Expression of sincere and specific thanks. People will see through disingenuous gratitude.
2. Acknowledgment of the effort or personal sacrifice made; it shows you are paying attention.
3. Statement about what it means to you personally. Expressing gratitude in this way is memorable, touching, and motivating.

Get people in the right seat on the bus.

It's not enough to have talent on your team; your employees must be in the right seat on the bus to do fantastic work. Great managers recognize that their employees will be at their best when their talents and strengths align with their roles. It takes time to gain meaningful insights into what makes your employees tick, but doing so will help you create, tweak, or change roles to help them do what they are best at every day. More tailored roles will result in happier, more productive and engaged team members who enjoy their work.

Rally teams around the bigger picture by tying it to the daily picture.

A job is just a job (aka a paycheck) when you can't see how it's tied to the bigger picture. Great managers understand that most of us want to be part of something greater than ourselves and tap into that motivation by ensuring every employee understands and cares about the company strategy and vision for the future. The key is tying strategy to a person's daily work, including well-thought-out and communicated departmental plans, key performance indicators (KPIs), work prioritization, and individual goals. Be transparent, talk about and get feedback on the vision and strategy often, engage more than just the usual suspects in vision and goal development, and celebrate small and big wins. The more connected your team is to the bigger picture, the greater your chance for success.

Be radically candid.

Great managers are always candid and address performance issues directly and timely. They show they care by being honest, compassionate, and holding their team accountable to high standards. They never take the easy way out by putting off tough conversations, sugarcoating bad news, or letting their desire to be liked to get in the way. They understand that every person on their team deserves to know how they are performing, what they need to do to improve, and how they are perceived within the organization. You cannot be a great boss without giving regular, candid feedback. Repeat this mantra over and over. If you want to get better at giving feedback, I highly recommend reading *Radical Candor: Be a Kickass Boss Without Losing Your Humanity* by Kim Scott. The book is a game-changer.

Practice your team's operating principles.

None of this will stick if you don't practice with intentionality. You must create a disciplined process for discussing your operating principles, surveying to discover where there is misalignment and creating commitments around them. We send out a quarterly survey and then build commitments around areas where we need to improve. We talk about how we embody the principles and lead our teams to do the same. We create goals, commitments, and tasks around the principles. This may seem like overkill, but trust me, it's not. To live and breathe them, you have to, well, live and breathe them.

• • •

Building a strong, high-functioning team is critical to your success as a leader. You can't build a great company without a stellar team that believes in the mission and works well together to execute the strategy and build a winning culture. If you don't have the right people on your team, address it immediately. The cost of an underperforming team or team member is always more significant than you think.

21

BE TRULY ACCOUNTABLE

Accountability is so much more than just admitting when you've made a mistake. Unfortunately, this is the narrow definition many people use, and they miss the bigger picture of true accountability. I am grateful to my mother for teaching me about accountability back in the ninth grade. I have carried this mindset of accountability forward, and it is a cornerstone in all that I do.

True accountability is fully owning everything that happens in your life. It means you understand you are responsible for your attitude, actions, reactions, teamwork, communication, and relationships. It also means you hold others accountable for the commitments and effort they give forth.

Early in my days as a CEO, I had a rocky relationship with a gentleman on my board of directors. I felt he was hypercritical and condescending, and I rarely felt supported by him. I secretly thought that he didn't believe I could do the job because I was a woman—and a young woman at that.

At the end of my first full year as a CEO, I negotiated my salary with the board. As you know, negotiating your salary is always nerve-wracking. But I was armed with data and prepared to ask for a significant increase. When I showed the compensation packages of CEOs in similar-sized companies, he replied, "You're not really a CEO." I was stunned. Then furious. Then hurt. That night, I cried myself to sleep. I blamed him for being chauvinistic and was determined to remove him from the board. The next day, I woke up and felt better and more rational. I knew that blaming him would make me a victim, and I refused to be a victim. Instead, I employed counterfactual thinking.

According to the American Psychological Association, counterfactual thinking is "any process of reasoning based on a conditional statement of the type 'If X, then Y' where X is known to be contrary to fact, impossible, or incapable of empirical verification." Basically, it's creating alternative thoughts or ideas about a past situation contrary to what actually occurred.

I knew that blaming him wouldn't reflect well on me, nor would it change the situation. I would still feel stuck and unhappy. So instead of trying to justify my feelings, I tried to see things from his perspective. Thinking in this new way allowed me to step back from my emotional response and consider a better path forward. I applied counterfactual thinking. I asked myself, *What if he's right? Am I acting and performing like an experienced CEO? Is it unreasonable for him to think that my jump from general manager to CEO was fast? Maybe I do have some things to learn. How do I approach this issue like a seasoned, professional CEO?*

Instead of being angry and vindictive, I called him to seek to understand better what he meant and why he said it. He apologized for his choice of words and shared that he thought I was a brilliant leader, just inexperienced. "I've been around the block a few times," he said, "and I know how hard it is to build a company. I want to support you, but it's not always easy. Sometimes you brush aside suggestions and minimize the difficulty of the road ahead, which comes across as defensive and a bit arrogant. I want to see you succeed, and one way to do that is to use the experience of your board as a competitive advantage rather than get defensive when we give you feedback."

Wow, what powerful feedback. I thanked him for his candor. In so many ways, he was right. Sure, his delivery was painful, but I didn't use poor delivery as an excuse not to own it. I made a significant shift in working with my board going forward and have a productive and healthy relationship with them. I use them as a competitive advantage. And I seek radically candid feedback from them and my team so that I stay humble and grounded.

This is what accountability looks like. When you choose to be accountable, you empower yourself to be part of a solution, building trust, resolving issues, and gaining a deeper understanding of yourself and those you work with. Being accountable feels better in the long run, even if it's a painful process because it builds self-esteem. There is nothing more powerful than solving your problems and fixing your mistakes.

You always have the option to let yourself be a victim of circumstance, giving away your power to change your situation, help your teammates, and solve your problems. Being a victim gives you an excuse to have a bad attitude, leading to poor relationships and spilling over into your relationships outside of work.

To me, there is almost nothing more important than responsibility and accountability. They lead to honesty, commitment, compassion, and integrity, and they build deeper, more fulfilling relationships. And you learn so much more by being accountable. The best way to describe accountability is to share some examples.

Put It into Practice:
How to Be More Accountable

Consider the following professional circumstances where individuals could choose to take accountability and control their course forward, or they can succumb to the circumstance and fall into victimhood.

You don't understand a decision your boss made. It's affecting your job, and you are losing sleep over it. What do you do?

How to be accountable in this situation: Seek to understand without blaming or making assumptions. Ask your boss about the decision; what was the background that triggered the decision, and how was it made? Is there a bigger picture that you aren't seeing? Then share how the decision is affecting you and offer solutions on how your stress might be eased.

How to NOT be accountable in this situation: Talk behind your boss's back but give them lip service to their face. Tell yourself that you can't change anything, so you'll just have to shut up and deal with it. Assume that it's their job to figure out how much the outcome is affecting the team; it was their decision, after all—now they must live with the consequences.

A peer shares with you that you come across as aggressive in meetings, and people are afraid to speak up in fear of being snapped at. What do you do?

How to be accountable in this situation: Say thank you for the feedback and ask more questions about how you are making people feel. Apologize to your peers. Ask them for help holding you account-able when you have an aggressive tone in meetings. Look within to understand why you are being aggressive; perhaps these meetings are ineffective and prolonged? Share your concerns, along with solutions, with your boss so she can help you come up with a plan to resolve issues that are negatively affecting your job. Ask for help if you don't have the tools or skills you need to communicate effectively.

How to NOT be accountable in this situation: Get defensive, make excuses, blame someone or something else, or otherwise blow off the feedback. Let your feelings get hurt so you shut down, refusing to talk or engage in meetings.

You've gone as far as you can go on a project, and you can't take the next step until a peer does their part, which doesn't seem to be happening. What do you do?

How to be accountable in this situation: Not wanting to make assumptions, you walk to their desk (or pick up the phone if you aren't in the same location; you know that sending an email could be miss-in-terrupted) and ask them how they are doing. Perhaps their boss gave them a different set of priorities, or they didn't know you were waiting on them. Ask them if there is anything you can do to help and when they expect to complete their portion. You tell them that you appreciate their workload and it's not your intention to pile on; you understand that you are both on the same team and succeed or fail together. At the end of the talk, you mutually agree on a timeframe. By doing this, you hold both yourself and your teammate accountable.

How to NOT be accountable in this situation: Take the mindset of "at least it's not on my desk anymore, so my boss can't blame me." You complain to other co-workers about your colleague behind their back but don't try to understand what's holding them up, nor do you give them feedback; it's not your problem nor your responsibility to make sure your teammates are doing their jobs.

There is a lot of miscommunication on your team. You are frustrated because everyone seems to be pulling in a different direction. What do you do?

How to be accountable in this situation: You ask your colleagues to sit down with you and assess what's happening. Why are you not all on the same page? Was there a breakdown in communication or process? What actions do we take to fix this? Ask for input from others. Develop a process to ensure better alignment. Present the plan to your manager as a solution to your problem. Commit to holding each other accountable to following the new process.

How to NOT be accountable in this situation: Grumble in frustration, ignore the issue, and feel resentful for the lack of progress. Decide not to speak up about the problem—your manager's job is to fix the team's poor communication issues.

You are having a rough morning, and it seems like everything that could go wrong does. You feel yourself slipping into annoyance and want to get snippy with your colleagues and direct reports. What do you do?

How to be accountable in this situation: You walk around the building to get some fresh air. You know your mood sets the tone for everyone around you, and you want to bring cheer, not gloom. While you walk, you think of all the things you are grateful for, understanding that a shift in mindset can help you shake the moodiness. You take a few deep breaths and walk back to your desk to write down three things that would help you get your day back on track. Then you stop by a colleague's desk and say, "I'm having a bit of a bad day. I am working hard to keep myself from spiraling into a bad mood, but I may need a pick-me-up. If I seem grumpy, can you please tell me a joke to help me smile?"

How to NOT be accountable in this situation: You let yourself fall into a bad mood and justify it by saying, "Everyone is allowed to have a bad day, and my team is just going to have to deal with it. I am in a bad mood because people are making mistakes and not communicating well. It's causing everything to go wrong." You avoid talking to your team, vowing to keep your head down and focus on getting your huge to-do list done. When someone comes and asks you a question, you give a short response and tell them that you are too busy to help.

• • •

In each of these examples, you had a choice: be accountable or not.

You can see when you choose to be accountable, you empower yourself to be part of a solution, building trust, resolving issues, and gaining a deeper understanding of yourself and those you work with. Being accountable feels better in the long run, even if it's a painful process because it builds self-esteem. There is nothing more powerful than solving your own problems and fixing your mistakes,

Or you can let yourself be a victim of circumstance, giving away your power to change your situation, help your teammates (including your boss), and solve your problems. Being a victim gives you an excuse to have a bad attitude, leading to poor relationships and spilling over into your relationships outside of work.

You get to choose every day: be empowered, or be the victim. What will it be?

22

BE CANDID WHEN GIVING FEEDBACK

Candidness is such a rarity today; maybe it always has been. We all say we want candor but tend to become defensive when we get it. Fear of negative reactions, conflict, and hurt feelings causes us not to want to be candid. But without it, so much goes unsaid, leaving missed opportunities to see new perspectives, course-correct, and improve.

What exactly is candidness? *Merriam-Webster* has an articulate yet straightforward definition: "the free expression of one's true feelings and opinions." Candidness is the quality of speaking with honesty, authenticity, and directness.

But in my (candid) opinion, what's missing from these definitions is that *effective* candor is a two-way street. It involves expressing your true feelings and opinions and listening and considering what others are saying. It's not about "just telling it like it is" and walking away. It's about engaging in meaningful conversation or debating topics that matter to those involved.

Candor is a dialogue, not an opportunity to stand on one's soapbox, pontificating, lecturing, or spewing hurtful opinions. When candor moves away from individual points of view, it opens the door to honest communication where you can explore meaningful, opposing, and even uncomfortable ideas and perspectives.

Candor is also important in driving performance. In her book *Radical Candor*, former Facebook executive Kim Scott says, "When bosses are too invested in everyone getting along, they also fail to encourage the people on their team to criticize one another for fear of sowing discord. They create the kind of work environment where being 'nice' is prioritized at the expense of critiquing and therefore improving actual performance." The goal is to give meaningful feedback which is specific, helpful, timely, and future-oriented.

If done well, you can move the needle in employee engagement. Gallup recently discovered that only 21 percent of US employees strongly agree that they have received meaningful feedback in the last week. Also according to Gallup, "Employees who receive daily feedback from their manager are three times more likely to be engaged than those who receive feedback once a year or less."[*]

Here's an example of candor done right.

One day during the pandemic, I was out for a walk, talking with an executive team member on the phone. In an obscure way, he asked my opinion about a continuous improvement issue. He hemmed and hawed and beat around the bush, clearly uncomfortable with the conversation.

"Are you okay?" I asked him.

"Yes, why?" he replied.

"Because I have no idea what you are trying to say," I said. "It's not

---

[*] "What Is Employee Engagement and How Do You Improve It?" Gallup, September 2022, https://www.gallup.com/workplace/285674/improve-employee-engagement-workplace.aspx.

like you to be this indirect, so I was wondering if you weren't feeling well. Or if you are trying to deliver bad news. Why don't you come out and say what needs to be said?"

He laughed. "I am trying to put my latest coaching session into practice. My team's feedback was that I need to let other people speak up and give their input before charging in with my ideas. So I decided to try it on you, but I was nervous, and I didn't know how you would respond!"

"Well, it was awkward and confusing," I teased him. "First, I am not the right person to practice this with. I don't want to give you my ideas. I want to hear yours. Second, it would be helpful if you let me know what you are practicing and why. Being a bit vulnerable about the feedback you received and your actions to correct your behavior will help others understand the sudden switch in style. They will be more open to helping you make positive changes. If you go about it this way, it will do more harm than good. You don't want to confuse people—or cause them concern. I thought you were having a stroke! With me, just be direct. Keep it real. Never beat around the bush."

The conversation that ensued was one of the most powerful I've had with him. We dove into his need to move quickly and make fast decisions. We brainstormed ways to be more present, ask better questions, and let others formulate their ideas and opinions. We laughed about him having a figurative stroke.

A few days later, he called to thank me for the feedback and the conversation. "I've never had a boss that I could speak to so candidly," he said. "Our conversation was incredibly motivating, and I feel like we understand each other better." I agreed. Our relationship grew stronger because of this candid discussion. In fact, he still talks about it regularly, expressing appreciation for how much it taught him.

Put It into Practice:
How to Be More Candid

It's simple: without direct, honest feedback, no one and no organization can improve. Clever ideas are left unexplored when people are too intimated to speak up and share their thoughts. Assumptions go unchallenged, leading to poor decision-making and failure to anticipate what might go wrong. A lack of straightforward communication affects every relationship and every organization. Candidness is essential to solving the problems we face on a day-to-day basis. Here are ways to be more candid:

Understand being candid is a personal choice.

No one can make you be candid. It's 100 percent up to you to decide whether or not you will engage in thoughtful, honest, mutually beneficial communication. Sure, some people make it easier to be candid than others, but ultimately, it's your responsibility. It might be messy at first—there is always a learning curve when you figure out how to effectively communicate with those you live with and work with, but it's worth the effort (and pain). Like any skill, candor takes practice and self-evaluation. When the delivery of your message isn't well-received, it may seem easier to shut down and clam up, vowing never to give feedback again, but this is the opposite of what you should do. Evaluate yourself. Was your tone too harsh? Did you have poor timing? Did you try to sugarcoat the message?

Learn how to be more candid
without damaging relationships.

We all fear being too candid. I get it; you don't want to hurt people's feelings or make them mad. People might call you a jerk and hold your words against you. You tell yourself a story of all the bad things that will happen if you are honest. These are all excuses. When done correctly, direct communication improves relationships, builds trust, and helps you be more successful. Here are some suggestions:

Be kind.

Candid feedback does not mean cruel feedback. Remember that the person in front of you is a human being (rather than an obstacle) with hopes, dreams, fears, and feelings, just like you. Being direct can be (and should be) done with compassion. Candor is not about attacking, blaming, shaming, or finger-pointing. It's about authentically sharing your thoughts and feelings to improve a situation. Be clear about your intentions, motivations, and objectives. Make sure they are in the spirit of building up rather than tearing down. That being said . . .

Don't beat around the bush.

Candor requires direct, straightforward speaking. Say what you think, say what you mean. Sugarcoating the message minimizes your impact, and it leads to misunderstandings. But . . .

Be objective.

Remember that what you are about to say is your opinion, and as much as it feels like the absolute truth, you might not have the whole story. You may be flat-out wrong. Being candid is about creating a dialogue; remaining objective helps keep the door open rather than slamming it shut. To do this . . .

Have specific examples.

The worst kind of feedback is unanchored feedback. Without specific examples to support your opinions, it's hard for anyone to gain deeper insight or take you as seriously as they could. Plus, without them, the person might become defensive. I'll give you an example: "I believe this is a bad idea," versus, "We don't have enough information to proceed. Recall the last time we made a knee-jerk decision? We had to undo six months' worth of work and start over. That's why I think this is a bad idea." And when the conversation is over . . .

Ask for feedback.

As I mentioned, being effectively candid takes practice, and the best kind of practice involves analyzing what went well and what went wrong. Plus, getting the opinions of others on your candidness allows you to get better at receiving feedback, showing that you genuinely value candor, even when someone is candid with you.

• • •

Make no bones about it. Candor doesn't come easily. As Jack Welch, the former CEO of General Electric, states in his book *Winning*, "We are socialized from childhood to soften bad news or to make nice about awkward subjects. People don't speak their minds because it's simply easier not to. When you tell it like it is, you can so easily create a mess—anger, pain, confusion, sadness, resentment." We must let go of these fears to become truly effective communicators. We must be willing to do the hard work.

In my experience, the deepest, most valuable relationships I have are with those who are candid with me and whom I am candid with in return. Effective candor = effective relationships.

23

LEAD WITH EMPATHY

Human beings are messy, emotional creatures. We all feel anxiety, anger, fear, and defensiveness at points in our lives, and often, we give in to these strong emotions. It gets even messier when we have emotional outbursts in the workplace, which can happen quite often.

At some point, every leader must handle a situation where an employee is angry or upset. How they deal with this emotional outburst is crucial to maintaining a positive working environment and, if done right, can positively change the trajectory of the employee's experience. But let's face it, it can be overwhelming to work through an emotionally charged situation with an employee, and it's easy to make things worse. The stakes are high, and a negative interaction could cause the employee to feel unheard or uncared about—decreasing overall satisfaction and possibly resulting in the person leaving the company. Being empathetic isn't just good for your employees, it's good for your career, too. According to a study by the Center for Creative Leadership, "Managers who show more empathy toward direct reports are viewed as better performers in their job by their bosses."*

Leaders need to approach human messiness with empathy, care, and some self-reflection. Leaders are flawed human beings, just like everyone else, but many are afraid to admit it. We have personal, family, and mental health issues. We, too, are messy. Sure, it's easy to hide behind statements like, "Everyone needs to leave their personal stuff at home," but who can really do that? And is it fair to expect people to not show up as their whole selves?

I am not saying that we shouldn't hold people to high expectations or tolerate bad behavior. But we can offer employees support and compassion as they go through messy times. I know I have benefited from kind leaders who helped me through my roughest periods.

Research agrees with me. According to a study performed by Catalyst, "76 percent of people with highly empathic senior leaders report often or always being engaged, compared to only 32 percent of people with less empathic senior leaders."

When people ask me if I would change anything about my checkered past, I unequivocally say, "NO!" My drug addiction opened my eyes to a different world, a different way of living. Without my addiction, I wouldn't understand that good people sometimes do bad things. I wouldn't know that bad people have beautiful qualities. I wouldn't know what it's like to royally screw things up, do things I am not proud of, and dig myself out of a hole so deep that I wanted to die. Nothing can replace the education I received on my way to hitting rock bottom.

These lessons are why when I received a phone call from a long-term employee, freaking out in Las Vegas when he was drugged and robbed

---

* "The Importance of Empathy in the Workplace," Center for Creative Leadership, November 28, 2020, https://www.ccl.org/articles/leading-effectively-articles/empathy-in-the-workplace-a-tool-for-effective-leadership/.

at a strip club, I helped him get home and initiate a lawsuit that took down a strip club crime ring.

These lessons are why when an employee called me from jail after getting his second DUI, I helped him get into counseling.

These lessons are why when an employee went through a horrible breakup, I hired a coach to help her heal her broken heart.

These lessons are why when an employee called to tell me she was having an affair with a colleague, I offered her support and wisdom, even though her decisions would limit her growth in the company and potentially cause drama within our organization.

These lessons are why when one of my executive team members told me that she was dreaming of early retirement, I hugged her and told her I would help her make it happen.

We are all messy, so instead of shunning the complicatedness of life, accept it with an open mind and a kind heart, balancing compassion with accountability. Appropriately connecting and communicating with an upset, traumatized, or troubled employee is essential to turn the situation around effectively.

Put It into Practice: How to Manage Highly Emotional Situations in the Workplace

Stay calm.

The best thing you can do is let the person be emotional and express his or her feelings. Take a few deep breaths to keep yourself from getting amped up. The last thing the person needs is for you to match his or her intensity or for you to try to end the conversation as quickly as possible because you feel uncomfortable.

Show concern and listen.

Make eye contact, lean forward, and listen to what the person is telling you. Avoid interjecting too soon. If the person is crying, hand them a tissue. Be personable and professional, show empathy, and don't judge or make the person feel bad about emotional outbursts.

Get to the facts.

Most people make incorrect conclusions about why a certain situation is happening, so it's essential to get to the facts. For example, if your employee says, "I can't deal with Larry anymore. He's condescending, and he is always picking apart my work. He's a jerk, and I am ready to walk out and never come back!" Your natural inclination might be to agree or disagree, but instead, try saying, "Tell me exactly what happened so I can understand the facts." Getting back to the facts helps others step away from their conclusion and provides you with the details you need to eventually resolve the problem.

Resolve the problem.

Once you get the facts and the person is calmer, let them know you want to help resolve the issue. Discuss a path forward, making specific agreements on how each of you will handle the situation. Be sure to have a clear follow-up plan so the issue doesn't go unresolved.

Keep it private.

Creating a scene is never helpful, so make sure you let the person have their emotional outburst privately. Move into a quiet office or go for a walk so that coworkers don't witness what's happening. Allow the

24

HELP OTHERS
FIND PURPOSE

I have found whenever I have been miserable at work, my life seems to go into quick decline. Early in my career, I didn't understand how devastating unmeaningful work and the wrong fit could be.

A big part of the reason my life began to spiral was that I was miserable at work. In my junior year at Mines, I was offered an internship at a Denver-based multi-disciplinary engineering firm. It paid incredibly well, and I had a fantastic boss whom I appreciate to this day, even though I still carry a bit of shame around the way I left him high and dry when I quickly left Denver in May 2002. After graduating from Mines, I took the path of least resistance and transitioned from intern to full-time employee at the firm. Truth be told, I had applied for several other jobs with big-name engineering and consulting companies but received no offers.

Looking back, I am sure those recruiters saw what I did not: I was an intelligent young woman who was lost and had no idea what she wanted to do. From an employer's perspective, it would take more work to train and maintain me than the value I would provide. I pretended I didn't care and accepted the offer from the company I was interning with without putting much more thought into it.

I understand now that your first job after college is about learning how to work as a proper adult. The work you do is important but less so than the skills and experience you gain in that first year. I am genuinely grateful for the experience, which included trips to Alaska to work on environmental projects at two military bases. My boss mentored and coached me, and I learned a lot, but I hated the work of calculating air quality and pollution emission rates and then writing reports on my team's findings. It's pretty much the opposite of my talents and interests, and I had no idea what I was doing. I constantly questioned myself, feeling like an imposter. *Am I adding value? Am I doing work that matters? What if my calculations are wrong? Why am I staring at another goddamned spreadsheet? I hate this!* Going to work drained me, and I dreaded getting on the express bus into downtown Denver every morning.

As you can imagine, my work situation inspired me to love after-work happy hours and going out on the weekends. This in itself is not unusual for a twenty-two-year-old, but disliking my job weighed on my psyche, and I began to lose perspective and balance. As you read earlier in this book, a few months after graduating, I started dabbling in drugs, mainly to numb my misery at work but also because it allowed me to push boundaries, a favorite pastime of mine. Underground raves on ecstasy and bumps of cocaine in the hottest nightclubs in town were not something a girl from rural Colorado and a graduate from Colorado School of Mines often did, at least not back then. Doing drugs made me feel sexy and cool—the opposite of what I usually felt: inadequate, awkward, and slightly overweight.

One Saturday night, while out with friends, I met a charismatic, funny, and cute man named Nate, who happened to be a friend of a friend. After the clubs closed, a group of us returned to Nate's place to continue the party. As the sun was rising, my friends and I called a cab to take us home, and I was smitten. He was everything I was not: plugged into the party scene, known by everyone, invited to all the parties, funny, chill, and . . . a drug dealer. The next day, Nate called and asked me out, and soon we were inseparable.

After a decade of working to understand my personality, triggers, and how I view self-preservation, I see how the combination of feeling like a fraud at work, wanting to be seen as cool and sexy, and my desire to push boundaries was dangerous. Dating Nate made me feel free. Suddenly, everyone knew my name. I was at the front of the line at the clubs and invited to the best parties. And I found out I could do a lot of drugs. Going out, getting high, and having fun was what I did; it was my life.

All the while, I went to work every day, no matter how hungover, which made me hate my job even more. I knew my performance was faltering, but I was too scared to ask for feedback or help. One day, I was still high and found myself in the office bathroom, using cocaine and crying. Things were getting bad.

Around that same time, the Enron scandal rocked the energy industry, and the company was laying off people across the country. My position was safe, but the guilt of staying in a job in which I was performing poorly (and quite frankly hated) while people around me were getting laid off was the push I needed to leave. I also needed to get out of Denver. Nate was in trouble due to drug deals that went sideways, and it seemed like a fresh start was in order.

I told my boss I was leaving; he was supportive and worried. He could tell things weren't good, but he never asked what was happening with me. I don't blame him for not wanting to get involved, but part of me was begging him to ask, "Are you okay? Do you need help?" Instead, he asked me to finish one final task before I left. Unfortunately, I didn't know how to complete the work, and I was too afraid of looking stupid to tell him. Instead of being honest, I left without doing it and, even worse, without acknowledging that I didn't do it. Drugs sucked the accountability out of me, among other things.

My life was out of control, and I was filled with shame. I moved to Austin, Texas, with Nate.

Leaving Denver was a good decision, but things got worse before they got better. And then worse again. It took me another year of serious drug abuse and scary situations to leave Nate. A stranger in my apartment with a gun and being sexually accosted by a paranoid friend were the two straws that broke the camel's back. While my life improved after I left Nate, I was still using drugs, albeit to a lesser extent.

When I got to Austin, I was hired as an operations coordinator for Eaton Corporation's electrical switchgear division. I loved this job. I was responsible for coordinating the electrical field engineering service group in Austin and San Antonio. It was like running a small business, and I had my fingers in everything, including billing, purchasing, and customer service. I learned about financial statements, variances, and manufacturing operations. I worked with a great group of engineers, but I had a terrible boss. He meant well, but I'm pretty sure he was addicted to painkillers, and when he actually showed up, he was out of it. I basically ran the operation but without a title or any authority. I couldn't have asked for a better experience; learning to manage through competence and influence shaped who I am today.

After two years in the job, I wanted to try sales. After talking to my boss, he let me dabble in it, which meant I could try sales on the side while keeping up my current duties. Which also meant that it would be next to impossible to succeed. But I was in my midtwenties and didn't know any better, so I decided to try it.

I didn't get anywhere, and soon I was passed up for an open sales position in Houston. My boss told me he didn't think sales was the right role for me because I hadn't made much traction in my part-time sales efforts. "It's just too hard for women to sell technical products," he said. His statement was demoralizing; I knew deep in my gut that I would be great at technical sales, and I decided to leave Eaton to take the next step in my career.

A few months later, I quit and successfully entered an entirely new field—high-end IT and software developer recruiting—to start my sales career as an account manager. I had no book of business, meaning I had no assigned accounts and had to develop all sales from scratch. By the end of the year, I was winning awards. My new boss was supportive, and I enjoyed what I was doing. It was hard work and every time I closed a deal, I knew I was on the right career path. I was on an upward trajectory, even though my private life was still quite messy.

And then I did something stupid. I quit, taking a higher-paying sales position at a different company. Six months into the new job, I was miserable again. The company, the role, and the leadership were a mismatch. I couldn't get any traction with new clients, and I felt like an imposter once again. I was too scared to ask for help because I had oversold my sales skills. "Just look at all the awards I've won" was my pitch to get the job, and I was embarrassed that I hadn't closed a deal in the first six months.

My personal life was also getting messier. I had just broken up with my boyfriend at the time, and I was using drugs more often and more heavily again. And then, because I was clearly crazy, I decided that competing in a figure competition was a good idea. A figure competition is a fitness contest that judges your physique, muscle tone, and posture. Body image issues have always plagued me, and I thought a body-building competition would help me lean out and build more confidence. It's safe to say analyzing everything that goes into your mouth and measuring your body every day while having a drug problem is a recipe for disaster. In a few short months, I found myself once again in a dangerous place.

I am grateful for being miserable at work, even though it led to self-destructive behavior. Both times it pushed me to make significant life changes that helped propel me to where I am today. A few months later, I swore that I would never allow myself to stay in a job that was not a fit for my skills, passion, and talents. But it took me almost dying alone to make that promise.

And yes, I did apologize to both my boss in Denver and the boss whom I left for a higher-paying job. It took me a few years, but I got my accountability back.

Why People Are Unhappy at Work

Before the pandemic, the job market was booming. Supposedly. A historic economic run showed job creation increasing, yet wages remained stagnant. In fact, the sentiment from the shrinking middle class was one of anger and resentment. For the first time in recent history, the hope that the next generation would create more wealth than the prior one diminished. Stuck in dead-end jobs that paid significantly less than what people felt they were worth, the working class grew frustrated with the lack of opportunity, the increasing income inequality, and, to put it bluntly, crappy benefits. The onslaught of the COVID-19 pandemic only highlighted these issues.

So why are people so unhappy at work?

In a comprehensive study performed by the Lumina Foundation, the Bill & Melinda Gates Foundation, Omidyar Network, and Gallup, researchers surveyed over 6,600 workers, asking them their views on what makes a "quality job," including compensation, benefits, the opportunity for advancement, job security and stability, and dignity. The findings were depressing but insightful and filled with all kinds of nuggets for improvement.

Over the past several decades, the American workforce has gone through a radical transformation. Globalization, automation, and the gig economy have changed the landscape for advancement and opportunity. While jobs have been created, it's questionable if they are high quality—ones that offer people satisfaction, meaning, dignity, and hope for a better future.

The study found that only 50 percent of American workers felt they were in quality jobs. Doing just enough to ensure they don't get fired, they don't contribute in ways that add value to the company and their own lives. The numbers are even more dismal for low-wage earners, and there was a strong correlation between unhappy workers in poor-quality jobs and race, ethnicity, and gender.

The results also showed that most people felt that the quality of jobs and opportunities for advancement had decreased. This leads to a lack of inspiration, loyalty, and engagement. People who felt they had bad jobs were twice as likely as those in good jobs to be looking for a new one. People unhappy at work are unhappy at home, too, compounding the effect of dead-end jobs. Across all participants, it was universal that everyone wanted a job that gave them a higher sense of purpose, not just a steady paycheck.

Understanding the Importance of Workplace Happiness

In the Gallup Organization's book, *Wellbeing: The Five Essential Elements*, the authors state that most people don't fully understand how important being happy in their jobs is to their overall well-being. But it makes sense. We spend most of our time working. We are introduced to others by what we do, such as, "This is Kerry Siggins, and she's the CEO of StoneAge." If your job drains you of energy, purpose, and dignity, it's hard to show up as healthy in the other four areas of well-being: social, financial, physical, and community.

In fact, Gallup found that people who rate their career well-being as being high are twice as likely to thrive in all areas of their lives. No matter what kind of physical shape you are in or how great your social life is, if you hate your job, you probably worry about it, complain about it, and dread getting out of bed to go to it.

CEOs and business leaders need to take heed. To create a strong company, you need strong managers to create strong teams. Strong teams require healthy, engaged employees who feel a sense of purpose, belonging, and being valued. Uninspired employees are unproductive and unhappy. Their energy is contagious, spilling over to other employees, and creating a toxic workplace. And when talent leaves, the toxicity only thickens.

If you want to be a leader who makes a significant impact on the world, you must start within your company first and create a culture that encourages engagement and a sense of purpose. You must work to create higher-quality jobs that lead to better opportunities and improved working conditions. You need to create an environment where employees are happy and can thrive.

Helping Your Employees Find Purpose

We all want to find meaning in our work. Employees look to their companies to help them find their way. While finding purpose is a personal and individual pursuit and can't be dictated or forced, companies need to assist their employees on their journeys to find purpose in meaning in what they do.

A recent McKinsey study found that 70 percent of the employees surveyed said their sense of purpose is largely defined by work. The importance of workplace well-being creates a significant opportunity to increase engagement and fulfillment throughout an organization. However, when the McKinsey researchers asked the survey participants if they lived their purpose at work, the results were interesting. Nearly 85 percent of executives and senior-level management said their work defines their purpose, but only 15 percent of frontline managers and individual contributors said the same. Even more disheartening, only 18 percent of respondents said they believed it was possible to find purpose in their work—at least to the desired levels.

The implications of these findings run deep and corroborate this data. The McKinsey report says, "These less satisfied respondents reported lower average work and life outcomes than more satisfied peers did— everything from reduced feelings of energy and life satisfaction to lower engagement, satisfaction, and excitement about work. Negative work and life outcomes for employees inevitably translate to negative outcomes for the business."

So, what does a leader do?

Putting It into Practice: How to Help Your Employees Find Purpose at Work

Start with what you can control.

During a recent conversation with a company I'm advising, I asked the CEO, "What's your vision for the company?" The response was to double the company's annual revenue for the next five years. Knowing this does not inspire a sense of purpose, I implored, "Why? Why is that your vision? And how do your employees respond when you say this?"

I've made this mistake, too; that's why it's easy for me to call out. While it may be exciting and financially rewarding to be part of a fast-growing company, most people are uninspired by a vision such as this. Why? Because it doesn't align with intrinsic values. Most people want to be part of something bigger than themselves. They want to make an impact in the lives of their customers, teams, and community. Start by clarifying your company's purpose and why their work makes a difference in the world. Then translate it to individual teams. Talk about it with your employees, asking them what resonates and what doesn't. Frequently survey them to ensure understanding and alignment. We do quarterly pulse surveys to check alignment and ask for feedback.

Talk about purpose.

The best way to draw out a personal purpose is to talk about it. According to the McKinsey survey, employees who can discuss how their personal purpose is tied to the company purpose are nearly three times more likely than others to feel fulfilled at work. Leaders need to create authentic ways to facilitate these discussions. I invite discussion through small, intimate town hall meetings with my employees and one-on-one breakout sessions at our monthly company meetings. It takes time and effort, but the results are worth it.

Hire and develop managers who care.

To create an environment where people feel comfortable sharing their purpose, you must cultivate it. And this starts with management.

Managers at every level must be willing to open up and share their own purpose and identify how and why it aligns with the company's purpose. Not everyone comes by this naturally; sharing personal stories is uncomfortable, and it's easy to dismiss this type of work as nonsense. First, start by hiring managers who understand and can demonstrate how their purpose aligns with the company's purpose. Don't be afraid to ask questions such as: What is your life's purpose? Have you had a job where you felt that your purpose and the company's purpose were in alignment? What was that like for you? How about when there was misalignment? What happened? Why does our purpose resonate with you? How will you help your team feel a sense of purpose at work?

Additionally, work with your managers closely, bringing them along on the journey, helping them articulate their life's vision and purpose, and coaching them to do the same with their employees. Make sure you discuss the company's purpose regularly and talk about how their teams create alignment around it. Brainstorm on ways you can improve. Employees need to feel a sense of ownership in the process if you want them to communicate about purpose with their teams effectively.

Help employees transition when there isn't alignment.

There are times when misalignment is unfixable, and that's okay. There's nothing wrong with admitting there's not a cultural fit. In fact, it's better to do so and to help the employee transition to another job at another company. Having transparent conversations allows for this to happen more organically, rather than letting feelings of unfulfillment and disenchantment create a toxic workplace for those who feel aligned.

• • •

If the Great Resignation taught us anything, it's that helping your employees find purpose in their work is the way of the future, at least if you want to build an employee-centric culture that attracts and retains talent. Talk about purpose and find ways to help your team find meaning in their work. You'll be a stronger company for it.

25

MOTIVATE YOUR EMPLOYEES

"Management is nothing more than motiving other people," said Lee Iacocca, who served as CEO of Chrysler Corporation in the 1980s. Sounds easy, right? Hardly. There is nothing easy about managing others. Lee is correct, though; great managers have an uncanny ability to tap into the motivations of others and use persuasive communication techniques to influence winning outcomes and high performance. Unfortunately, too many managers have no idea how to motivate their teams effectively.

I learned about a leader's impact on motivation the hard way. Early in my career, I had a boss who had no idea how to tap into the motivations of his employees. He was a good person but lacked the skills and confidence to motivate us. He showed little interest in my personal development and used scare tactics to try to influence me. After a while, I saw through it. He was ineffective and uninspiring. Eventually, the company fired him, and I vowed that if and when I was a manager, I would never lead like him.

So, where do well-intentioned but ineffective managers go wrong?

A study published by *The European Journal of Business and Management* found that employees who are regularly recognized and shown appreciation are more motivated to do their jobs well. Positive feedback and recognition creates more enthusiasm, energy, and commitment. Employees who put the company's best interest first saw increased growth opportunities and the ability to earn more income. Companies that create structures and policies that encourage and support employee recognition and empowerment are more likely to succeed, correlating employee motivation and organizational effectiveness.

Daniel Pink, author of *Drive: The Surprising Truth About What Motivates Us,* agrees. He says that once people are paid fairly for their jobs, they are motivated by the need for autonomy—the desire to be self-directed; mastery—the desire to develop our skills; and purpose—the desire to do meaningful and purposeful work. Pink states, "Motivation 1.0 presumed that humans were biological creatures, struggling to obtain our basic needs for food, security, and sex. Motivation 2.0 presumed that humans also responded to rewards and punishments. That worked fine for routine tasks but was incompatible with how we organize what we do, how we think about what we do, and how we do what we do. We need an upgrade. Motivation 3.0, the upgrade we now need, presumes that humans also have a drive to learn, to create, and to better the world."

I know this to be true, as my job allows for autonomy, mastery, and purpose. I work hard to create this for my employees, too. It's why we created the Own It Mindset, which weaves these three pillars of motivation into how we show up as employees, how we train our managers, and how we deliver on our purpose as a company: to help our customers do their jobs safer and more efficiently so they can go home safely to their families every night. Aiding our employees on their self-leadership journey is crucial, and it takes commitment from both the company and the employee. When combined with recognition and empowerment, self-leadership leads to autonomy, mastery, and purpose; it's not one-sided.

An excellent example of promoting self-leadership is how I work with my executive team. Using our commitment processes and holding ourselves accountable to our operating principles, we've created a team built on autonomy, mastery, and purpose. They understand that together, we *all* run the company, not just me as the CEO. Each team member works toward the vision with a clear set of goals and commitments. It's up to each of them to get their jobs done in a collaborative, dynamic way. I set the tone, help course-correct when needed, provide support and training, and then let them do their thing. Each of them finds purpose in their work for different reasons—their purpose is a very personal thing—but they all have it, whether it's creating products that save lives, developing a plan that allows for better execution of our strategy, creating efficiencies that help our employees do their jobs easier, or hiring great teammates who add to our engaging and powerful culture. The secret sauce is that every person knows they are cared about—by me and by each other. We help each other, support each other, and have fun together—all while working hard.

A text I received from one of my executives is burned in my memory forever. He sent me a picture of the view from his house as he was relaxing outside with this family with a note that said, "None of this would be possible without StoneAge. Not this house, not my life, not my marriage, not my career. Thank you for everything you've done to help me grow. I promise to give you 100 percent of my commitment and effort every day."

That is what motivation looks like, and it motivates me as a leader. I read that text whenever I feel like I am taking two steps backward for every step forward.

Put It into Practice:
How to Motivate Your Employees

Allow employees to control how they do their work.

Many managers believe they will save time if they tell their teams how to get things done. This kind of micromanagement is frustrating and demoralizing, as most employees want to be more self-directed and have the autonomy to make choices about their work. Great managers motivate their teams by clearly defining success, removing roadblocks, course-correcting when needed, and otherwise getting out of the way.

Talk less, listen more.

Truly hearing people is essential, and good managers know how to ask the right questions to draw out meaningful and informative dialogue. Make your employees feel valued by asking questions such as, "What do you suggest?" or "I'd like to hear your opinion; what do you think?" Most people will give you clues to what motivates them if you stop talking long enough to hear what they are trying to tell you.

Hold regular tag-ups.

In today's world of too many meetings, it's easy to blow off weekly tag-ups with each employee. Don't do this. Most people find interaction with upper management to be motivational. Encourage your team members to come prepared with work-clarifying questions, problem-solving ideas, requests for information, and information that keeps you in the loop.

Share the why.

Managers who fail to share meaningful information with their teams will fail to motivate them. People want to feel like they are "in the know" and important enough to be informed about what is happening within the organization and, more importantly, why it's happening. Be transparent, ask for feedback, and always share the why behind actions and decisions. More about this in the next chapter.

Recognize contributions.

Great managers know they must consistently recognize contributions and show appreciation. Tell your employees when they've done a good job. Notice and comment on their incremental improvements, not just the big ones. Send weekly thank you notes to people throughout your organization. Set up a peer-based recognition system. Just be timely, consistent, and specific.

Deal with issues in the workplace.

Many managers don't know how to effectively deal with conflict, performance issues, and other morale-sucking behaviors. Failing to listen to and address these issues will turn your best performers into mediocre ones; therefore, commit to effectively handling employee complaints. Keep the feedback loop healthy by providing regular updates on how you are addressing their concerns. Ask them to be part of the solution and give you feedback on what isn't working. This shows your team that workplace problems don't fall into a black hole, and it's safe to bring up problems.

Create growth opportunities.

Motivating people is hard if they feel like they are in dead-end jobs. Give your employees opportunities to expand their skills and take on new challenges. Allow your employees to attend important meetings, let them cross-train in other functions, give them special projects, and encourage them to participate in external seminars and courses. Ensure each team member has a career development plan that outlines their long-term goals and plans to help them get there.

• • •

Doing these things will increase motivation within your team, and everyone will reap the benefits. With motivated and engaged employees who contribute real value to the organization, you'll be more likely to achieve your goals and be successful.

26

SHARE THE WHY

Fear is one of the most destructive emotions in the workplace. When we come from a place of fear, we are more likely to be defensive, find fault in others, blame ourselves, and tell ourselves a story about that fear that is most likely inaccurate. We tend to focus on fear rather than doing more beneficial things such as completing a task or building a relationship. Moreover, there probably isn't a single person in your organization who doesn't feel fear each day, or its close cousins, worry and anxiety. Fear, if not overcome, is unhealthy because fear robs people of their potential and creates a stressful and unproductive work environment.

In my experience, change is one of the biggest drivers of fear. Even though we experience change constantly, we fight it tooth and nail. Our brains expect certain things to stay the same, and when they don't, the information we trust has broken down, causing us fear over what comes next. What we don't know tends to scare us, and change creates a lot of unknowns.

That's why, as a leader, it's so important to explain the *why*. The why behind the change gives people context and helps them understand the reason behind *what* is changing. Once the brain knows the why, it can start building a new story that is more accurate and less intimidating.

Plus, workplace transparency leads to long-term business success. According to Glassdoor, "when implemented properly, increased transparency creates trust between employers and employees, helps improve morale, lowers job-related stress, while increasing employee happiness and boosting performance. And being transparent costs nothing, which gives it an exceptional ROI."*

I learned a hard lesson about not sharing the why when planning to change our business model and go direct to our customers. As I shared previously, the stakes were high. We were moving fast and didn't want anyone in the industry to get wind of what we were doing. So, the executive management team holed up in a conference room, dubbed "The War Room," and mapped out our game plan. We decided to lock the door at night so no one could come in and see our whiteboards filled with ideas and decisions. We told our employees that this was top secret and we wouldn't share the plan until we had it figured out. These covert actions were a departure from how we normally did things. We are an open-book company and share our financials and strategy with everyone in the company. The lack of transparency scared people.

They wondered what we were doing and began to question if we were making good decisions. It quickly brought about distrust in the process, and people felt left out and in the dark. In fact, on an employee survey a few months later, someone described feeling like a mushroom, left in the dark and fed poop.

The damage took a while to undo. I asked people to go through heroics to execute the plan, and the process disgruntled several people. I vowed never to operate that way again.

---

* "Transparency in the Workplace: Why It Matters and How to Practice It," Glassdoor, June 29, 2021, https://www.glassdoor.com/employers/blog/transparency-in-the-workplace/.

I appreciate what Glassdoor has to say about workplace transparency. "Self-preservation is a powerful instinct. The knowledge that the truth isn't always pleasant means that even as adults, many of us hold back when transparency might make us vulnerable. We're taught that honesty is the best policy, but that if we have nothing nice to say, it's best to say nothing at all. But transparency isn't about throwing caution to the wind or blurting out whatever comes to mind; it's about understanding the benefit of honest and forthright communication in your organization. Knowledge is power, and the lesson to take away is that transparency, truth, and openness spread knowledge that empowers people and businesses to do better work together."

Put It into Practice: How to Share the Why

Write out the why.

Along the way, I've learned that just because you share the why doesn't ensure everyone understands it. Speaking articulately and accurately in front of an audience, in meetings, or one-on-one can be challenging. You must think about the meaning and tone behind your words and understand who your audience is and what will resonate with them. Something that has helped me, especially in crucial conversations where change is significant and stakes are high, is to write out what I am going to say. I write out every word I want to say. This tactic may or may not work for you but at the very least, write a bullet point list of what you want to convey.

Think about the who, what, when, and how of the why.

People care about the details, and they always start by wondering *What does this mean for me?* As you formulate your message, start with who first. Who is your audience, and what do they care about? What message will they hear versus what message are you communicating? What concerns will they have? Then outline the what, describing the situation and its impact on the organization. Next comes the when: Is there a sense of urgency? When will the change take place? How long will it last? Follow up with the how: here's how we will get there and the outcomes we would like to see.

Anticipate where things could go wrong.

Another important step is to try to predict questions, concerns, and pushback so you can either work them into your dialogue in advance or so you are prepared when someone speaks up. Anticipating where things could go wrong is often overlooked—especially by overly optimistic people. But identifying obstacles and pushback can not only help you be ready to think on your feet, but the foresight helps you come up with a plan to overcome them. Doing this enables you to prepare to deliver a compelling *why* message.

Follow up to ensure understanding and alignment.

Lastly, commit to following up with whomever your audience is. What you say and what people hear are often very different. It's essential to follow up even when the *why* message isn't high-stakes. Remember that different things trigger different people. You might want to tweak a person's role slightly, and he might hear that his entire job is changing.

He immediately stops listening because his brain goes into "fear of change" mode. He may nod, act like he understands, and then walk away, anxious, and angry. Following up can be as simple as waiting a day and asking if he has thoughts or concerns about the discussion. Make time to sit in a quiet space and listen intently to what he has to say. Ask questions to get to the heart of the matter.

• • •

If you do one thing as a manager or leader, share the why as often and openly as possible. Even if it seems benign, people *always* want to know the *why* behind what they are doing. It makes them feel in the know, part of the solution, and safer, increasing engagement. And companies where employees are highly engaged are 21 percent more profitable than those who have less engaged employees—a compelling reason to be transparent.*

---

*   "8 Employee Engagement Statistics You Need to Know in 2022," HR Cloud, June 9, 2022, https://www.hrcloud.com/blog/8-employee-engagement-statistics-you-need-to-know-in-2021#:~:text=A%20Highly%20Engaged%20Workforce%20Increases,companies%20with%20a%20disengaged%20workforce.

27

NURTURE
ROCK-STAR EMPLOYEES

One afternoon, I had a conversation with a bright young woman about her deep desire to realize her potential. Her current job was a fit for her skills, talents, and career goals in some ways, but she felt underutilized in others and that several of the job requirements weren't a good match. She loved working for StoneAge, but she believed that her immediate career path was limited because there wasn't a clear role for her to move into. It was hard for her to see the possibilities of what didn't yet exist. No job description, no open position, no job growth—right?

But the fact is that companies create new jobs every day. At companies across the globe, positions are being established as leaders implement new strategies, enter new markets, create new business models, and develop new technology. And forward-thinking companies are creating new roles explicitly designed for competent people, fully utilizing their talents and helping them reach new potentials. They are upskilling their team members, preparing for the future of work where artificial intelligence (AI) is omnipresent.

Marcus Buckingham and Curt Coffman's book *First Break All the Rules: What the World's Greatest Managers Do Differently* inspired me early in my management career. In the book, they explain how the best managers select an employee for talent rather than skills or experience and motivate them by building on strengths rather than focusing on weaknesses. Focusing on talents leads to high performance, deep engagement, and what I like to call "rock star" employees.

This message resonated deeply with me. I wanted nothing more than to be a great manager and create an environment where "rock stars" could invent themselves and thrive. To do this, I had to learn more about my employees. What motivated each of them? What parts of their job did they love? Hate? What were their personality styles? What caused them to step up and take on new challenges or, the opposite, retreat? At what did they excel, and when did they underperform? What would be the perfect role? Over the last decade, I've trained myself to see the talents of others and ask the right questions to reveal fears, desires, talents, capabilities, motivations, and weaknesses.

With this knowledge, I can then either modify or create new roles that fit their unique set of talents and better guide them as they grow in their careers. Doing this has led to new opportunities within the organization, and we have happier, more engaged employees who enjoy their jobs because they get to do what they are good at every day.

Going back to the young woman who felt she had no options but to leave the company—we went through this process together and brainstormed where her talents and the needs of the company intersected. We created a new role for her, taking some of her current job's responsibilities and adding new ones that better fit her talents and goals. Within the first month, it was clear that she was thriving. She was happy and more engaged, excelling in her new position and taking on more than we originally outlined in the new job description. She still works for us today and has been promoted to a senior management role.

Engaged employees help cultivate a positive culture, and it's well-known that great workplace cultures lead to higher productivity and retention. According to research by Gallup, people who use their strengths every day are six times more likely to be engaged on the job.[*] This data is a compelling reason to tailor your job descriptions. Because of the success we've had, I am a big believer in designing roles for our employees, especially those who have high potential and demonstrate the desire to grow personally and professionally. I have seen how powerful moving an underperforming yet highly capable person into a better-suited position can be. Over and over, it has made a profound impact on the company's performance. Employees are happier because they are thriving, motivated, engaged, and doing enjoyable tasks, and they're well on the way to rock stardom.

All of this sounds great. But how do you do it? How do you deeply understand your employees and position them in the right roles?

Put It into Practice:
Align Employee Talents with Their Roles

Use personality and work-style assessments to help recognize motivators, strengths, talents, and preferences.

We use social styles as a basic foundation because the styles are easy to remember and understand. There are four basic styles: analytical, driver, amiable, and expressive. Social style tendencies are easy to spot,

---

[*]   Susan Sorenson, "How Employees' Strengths Make Your Company Stronger," Gallup, accessed September 2022, https://www.gallup.com/workplace/231605/employees-strengths-company-stronger.aspx.

and you can do some fun teambuilding around them. We also use the Predicative Index© and the TTI DISC© profile assessment, potent tools that summarize primary personality characteristics that describe, explain, and predict day-to-day workplace behaviors. These tools can be costly but are worth the investment, as they will give you and your employees valuable insight into what makes them tick and how to set themselves up for success.

Get to know your employees personally.

Understanding their motivations, goals, struggles, and family situations aids you in seeing your employees more holistically. It will give you deeper insight into strengths and weaknesses, helping you steer them into ideal roles. Plus, it's easier to transition someone into a different position with a strong personal connection when there is more trust in the relationship.

Help your employees determine and understand their strengths, and talk about how their current positions fit those strengths.

Most people don't know their strengths (and neither do their managers), so I recommend using the Strengths Finder assessment to start the process. Gallup's data shows that employees will be 7.8 percent more productive when they understand their strengths. Even more convincing, teams that focus on strengths every day have 12.5 percent more productive. We all have parts of our job that aren't as satisfying as others, and the goal isn't to create jobs filled only with enjoyable tasks. But you do want to look for evident talent/job mismatches. Do you have a highly analytical person working in a position that requires her to live in the gray area? Do you have an empathetic peacemaker in a role that requires him to play devil's advocate? Do you have a person who gets tongue-tied when giving performance reviews in a management role? Do you have a strategic thinker doing repetitive tasks? Do you have someone who thrives on connecting with her coworkers in a position with little interaction?

Take the time to evaluate the performance of each employee, and do it often.

Observe them in action, review the quality of their work, get feedback from peers and direct reports, and listen to their communication tone and style. Discuss these observations regularly, guiding them to find what they truly enjoy and course-correct issues in real-time. Doing so will bring more awareness to strengths and weaknesses and allow you to openly discuss which duties and responsibilities best suit each employee.

Don't be afraid to modify job descriptions.

It's tempting to have a standard job description and tell yourself that you must find the right person to fit that exact role. But this is hardly realistic or sustainable. Each role changes as the company changes, so be flexible in ways that make sense for the company and the employee. This approach does not require that you create unique job descriptions for everyone on your team. It simply means having an open mind to modify some responsibilities to match people's strengths better. In some cases, it might make sense to create a whole new role. Good talent is hard to find, and if the job is a poor match, it's better (if possible) to craft a new job to keep a person rather than watch them get frustrated, fail, and leave.

• • •

It takes time, commitment, and some trial and error to get to know your employees, especially in the context of true strengths. I've had great success developing employees by modifying and creating roles—as well as some failures. I have become too emotionally invested in helping struggling employees find the right roles within the organization. It's painful on both sides when it's time to admit that there isn't a fit that mutually works. But the time, energy, and emotion spent trying are worth it. Engaged and happy employees in roles based on their strengths and talents make the employee, organization, and you better. I believe there is no worthier use of my time than spending it to sincerely understand and appreciate my team's strengths and talents, helping them become rock stars.

28

LEAD IMPACTFUL PERFORMANCE CONVERSATIONS

When asked what I think is the most important thing a leader can do to develop his or her people, I give a simple answer: a good leader is committed to developing their employees, which means they consistently provide meaningful performance feedback. And by always, I don't mean once a year during an annual performance evaluation.

Every employee in your organization deserves to know where they stand at all times. That's why the dreaded annual evaluation process doesn't work. A once-a-year discussion with an employee about her goals and performance isn't motivating, nor does it change behavior. In fact, Gallup reported that only 14 percent of employees feel that their annual performance review inspires them to grow. Therefore, the traditional annual review is a waste of time and must go.*

---

* John Knotwell, "5 Ways to Have More Effective Performance Conversations," Reworked, August 25, 2020, https://www.reworked.co/learning-development/5-ways-to-have-more-effective-performance-conversations/.

I recall my first annual performance review in my early twenties . . . it was awful. Even though I was performing quite well, I left uninspired and a bit deflated. The scoring system felt arbitrary, the comments were superficial, and my goals had nothing to do with reality. My boss checked a box, and then we all got back to work. The reviews didn't get much better as I changed jobs. When I came to StoneAge, the management team did something similar, and I vowed to change it. But how?

After researching what other companies were doing and being inspired by a leadership consultant, we created what we now call "Own It Chats," employee-led, quarterly performance conversations. Own It Chats create regular opportunities for managers and their employees to talk about what is and isn't going well, discuss progress on goals and initiatives, and give each other feedback. They allow managers to keep their pulse on cultural issues because we always ask questions about trust, connection, gratitude, and self-leadership.

Most of my employees look forward to these performance conversations because they get to lead the conversation, receive recognition as well as course corrections, and know exactly where they stand by the end of the conversation. While it takes time for managers to hold these chats, it ensures alignment and helps them address issues they normally wouldn't. Own It Chats are documented for easy reference, which is helpful when performance issues are recurring. Overall, the feedback from employees is positive and powerful—they feel more connected and at ease after their quarterly performance conversations.

Put It into Practice: Create a More Meaningful Performance Conversation

Each quarter meet with your employees to discuss what's going well and what isn't and create an action plan for career development and improvement. These meetings are also an excellent opportunity to ensure your employees are working on the *right* things—work that aligns with strategy execution and is of high value to the company.

Prompt direct reports to prepare for the meeting.

To prepare for these performance discussions, ask each employee to write out their answers to these five questions:

1. What do you feel you are doing well?
2. What do you feel you aren't doing well?
3. What are the two most important things you are working on right now?
4. What can I do to help you improve or do your job better?
5. What feedback do you have for me, the team, or the company?

Once they have provided you with their responses, add your comments. Be sure to highlight examples of things you've seen going well and give candid feedback on what can be improved, even if it seems insignificant. Even the most minor course correction can yield significant results. Analyze their responses to the third question about what they are working on right now. Notice I didn't ask, "What are your top two priorities?" Priorities don't always tie to what an employee is doing, which is a problem. You need to ensure that they spend their time on the *right* tasks, ensuring that their goals align with the company strategy. This approach is far more effective than setting goals once per year. Lastly, don't overlook the fourth question. Even if they say that you can do nothing to help them improve, dig a bit more. Ask if there are things you do that get in the way or make his job harder. Don't be satisfied with a non-answer. Getting feedback from your employees is how you improve your performance and theirs.

But this takes so much time, you say? Yes, it does, but the results you get from giving regular feedback far outweigh the time it takes to sit down for forty-five minutes and talk about performance each quarter. I can promise you this: your employees need and want feedback; they crave it, both good and even the bad. According to a study performed by Jack Zenger and Joseph Folkman, published in the *Harvard Business Review* article titled "Your Employees Want the Negative Feedback You Hate to Give," 92 percent of respondents said the "negative feedback, if delivered appropriately, is effective at improving performance." The awareness helps them get better at their jobs, which is good for you as a manager. Plus, what could be more important than helping your employees improve? People are your greatest asset, and rock-star employees make a company successful. Your number one goal should be to develop as many stars as possible.

Facilitate quarterly meetings even if you can't overhaul your company's performance review process.

But I can't influence my company's annual performance review process, you say? I say, "So what?" Follow the process anyway. It will make your job easier at the end of the year when you must prepare the annual evaluation; you'll have four documented performance conversations to refer to. And you'll have motivated and productive employees because they are getting regular, meaningful feedback throughout the year. And suppose you have an employee with continuous performance issues with little corrective action. In that case, it'll be easier to manage him into another role or out of the company because you'll have plenty of documented conversations to back up your decision. HR will love you for this!

Initiate feedback conversations outside of regular meetings.

Don't wait for your quarterly meetings to give feedback. Receiving it real-time allows employees to see more clearly how their behavior or effort affects their performance, especially when it's tied to a specific instance. For example, if an employee checks her phone during a meeting, pull her aside and ask about her inattentiveness. It's essential to understand why she's exhibiting the behavior before jumping into the feedback. This will give insight into what's going on without making her defensive. Then share with her that both you and the team don't feel that she is engaged when she's not actively participating, and this hurts her ability to be an effective teammate and it causes her to be perceived as unhelpful. Help her develop a plan to solve her issues around why she wasn't participating to actively engage and be a better teammate. This is highly effective; it would have lost its punch if you had waited to share it until the next performance conversation. In fact, you probably would have blown it off and not said anything. Doing it in real time allows her to make immediate changes, and it gives your insight into an issue she was struggling with, allowing you to help her move past it. This is excellent management.

• • •

According to LinkedIn's 2020 Workplace Learning Report, 90 percent of professionals say they would stay longer at a company that invested in their growth.* Frequent performance conversations, when done well, facilitate the growth your employees are looking for and increase engagement and retention—top priorities for you as a leader.

---

* "2022 Workplace Learning Report: The Transformation of L&D," LinkedIn Learning, accessed September 2022, https://learning.linkedin.com/content/dam/me/learning/en-us/pdfs/workplace-learning-report/LinkedIn-Learning_Workplace-Learning-Report-2022-EN.pdf.

29

RECOGNIZE THE POWER OF TRANSPARENCY

We all know that trust is the key to any successful relationship. There are many ways to build trust, but one of the most impactful ways is to be transparent. If you aren't transparent, creating the long-lasting relationships you desire will be much more difficult.

While transparency is essential in all relationships, it's the cornerstone of businesses that want to create a culture of happiness, engagement, high performance, and mutual respect. Employees in any organization have a deep desire to know what's going on and why. They want to give input and be heard. They don't want to fear the future and be scared of change. But the only way to reduce fear and motivate them to be their best is to be transparent. According to Calum Smeaton, founder and CEO of UK-based AdTech company TVSquared, "Employees need to know both the good and the bad" about the company's status. "If you're not transparent, that's where you create a breeding ground for insecurity."*

What is transparency in business? One business dictionary defines it as a "lack of hidden agendas or conditions, accompanied by the availability of full information required for collaboration, cooperation, and collective decision-making." Simple enough concept to understand, but how do you do it?

In February 2020, StoneAge experienced a ransomware encryption attack. On a cold, snowy Saturday morning, I got a call from our IT manager saying that our entire IT infrastructure was shut down. I rushed to the office and joined the IT team as we tried to figure out what was happening. After hours of digging, we found the ransomware note, giving us instructions on contacting the hackers to pay the ransom. I freaked out. How did this happen to us? We are just a small company in rural Colorado. I soon learned that size and location have nothing to do with why hackers target a company.

Later that evening, I asked twenty-five employees to come to work Sunday morning. At 8:00 a.m., we were sitting at the conference room table, and they looked at me with fear in their eyes. I felt their fear, too. This was bad.

I told them what we knew so far. "We've been hacked, and none of our IT and software systems are accessible. We are essentially locked out of everything," I said. "We have hired a forensic and negotiating team. They, along with the IT team, will be figuring out what we lost and whether we will have to pay the ransom to get it back. This is a big deal because it's our busiest time of year, and our customers can't feel a thing. We must figure out a way to keep shipping product and do it so that it doesn't wreak havoc on our system when we have to manually log

---

* May Teng, "A Lack of Transparency Creates a 'Breeding Ground of Insecurity,' According to One Tech CEO," *Insider*, March 15, 2021, https://www.businessinsider.com/why-transparent-leadership-is-critical-during-times-of-crisis-2021-3.

it in our digital systems once we're back up and running. The twenty-five of you have all day to figure out what we are going to do. Tomorrow at 8:00 a.m., I will hold a company meeting to let everyone know what's going on and how we will handle this."

They went to work, and due to their commitment and genius, they devised a system to track, pack, and ship orders.

The next morning at 8:00 a.m. sharp, the company gathered around as I told them what had happened. "We are in uncharted waters," I said gravely. "But we have a plan. I know that we can pull this off. All we have to do is work together, follow the process, iterate as we learn, and do everything we can to not pay the hackers!" The whole company cheered. "I promise you I will share everything that happens as we go through this process," I continued. "You will know what I know, and we will get through this together."

And you know what? We did get through it. Our response was the most outstanding example of teamwork I have ever seen. Standing shoulder to shoulder, we manually shipped all but four orders over four weeks. In fact, we had our biggest week ever, shipping over $1 million dollars in products in a week—manually. Our customers didn't feel a thing, and the camaraderie was palatable. You could feel the energy as we worked together to get through the biggest crisis we had faced as a company. And I kept my promise. At the end of each day, I sent an email update, letting people know where we stood and the progress we had made. They knew everything I knew, and we were able to rebuild without paying the ransom.

I learned just how motivating transparency could be.

Put It into Practice: How to Be More Transparent

Have a true open-door policy.

As a leader, it's easy to say you have an open door, but if you don't have anyone walking into your office to ask hard questions, give you feedback, discuss strategy, or share concerns, your open-door policy isn't working. It's difficult for employees to bring up issues, so you must do everything you can to make them feel comfortable doing so. Never get defensive; listen closely, ask questions, take action, follow up, and always say thank you.

If your employees aren't proactively coming to you, invite them in to talk. Ask easy questions at first. Say things like, "I get the feeling that a lot of people aren't speaking up about some of the issues we have here. I need some insight so I can make things better. Can you tell me what you see?" You will probably get a softened truth as the person feels you out, but this is how you build better relationships with your employees. If you handle yourself appropriately, take action, and be consistent, you will begin to see people taking advantage of your open-door policy and your organization becoming more transparent.

Get out of your office.

Don't expect everyone to come to your office; take your open-door policy to them. Walk around the facility and talk to employees, even those who report to other managers. Ask questions about their work, their issues, and what they need to do their jobs better. Give them updates on what's going on in your department. Share a customer story. Tell them about an issue you are dealing with and ask for their opinions. Even better, ask people to go for a walk. There is something magical about walking meetings, and it's a great way to share and learn

• • •

During a study performed by HR Science Forum, researchers learned that transparent organizations are more productive, innovative, and considered to be trustworthy by their employees. In building a high-performing organization, transparency is essential. It takes time to build trust, so take it slow and be authentic. Be honest about your efforts to be more transparent. Ask your employees for feedback and to commit to being more transparent themselves. Be forthright with information, keep your promises, and always tell the truth. It's a worthy endeavor as employees who feel like they are in the loop and can voice their opinions are more likely to be engaged, happy, and productive.

30

DEAL WITH
DIFFICULT PEOPLE

We all have high-maintenance people in our lives. You know the person who is never satisfied, never stops talking, makes snippy comments, doesn't follow the process, or is the narcissist who is always right? No matter where you work, you'll have to deal with those who make things harder than they have to be. While it may seem like your life would be better if you didn't have to deal with people like this, challenging people can make things better in an organization.

In a 2016 survey conducted by Weber Shandwick, 30 percent of managers confirmed that they had fired or threatened to fire someone due to toxic workplace behaviors, and nearly 25 percent of employees said they had quit a job due to an uncivil workplace. Additionally, 87 percent of respondents said that disruptive an uncivil behavior negatively impacted theirs and their colleagues' performance. Dealing with toxicity in the workplace is one of the most important tasks you have as a leader.

Humans solve problems; that's why we are all so different. We each see the world through our unique lens and bring diverse perspectives to the table. In the workplace, having different and even opposing opinions is critical to good decision-making. While it may "feel" better to have peace and harmony, it's not ideal. Conflict is good when handled appropriately because it forces a team to look at all the possibilities. Conflict should be encouraged and managed.

I once had a manager working for me who was rigidly black-and-white in outlook and somewhat introverted; he struggled with our fast pace and our less-than-robust processes. Incredibly dramatic facial expressions often left people wondering why he was always so angry, and I heard several complaints about how difficult he was to work with. After a few conflicts arose, I asked if he knew how he looked when he had an intense conversation.

"No," he said. "Why?"

"Your face scrunches up, and your eyes narrow when you are thinking about what you want to say or when the conversation isn't going the way you want to go," I replied. "It's causing conflict in meetings because people feel you are being passive-aggressive. You say one thing, but your face is saying something entirely different. Do you notice people are getting defensive and that meetings devolve because people want to leave?"

"Yes," he said, "but I don't understand why."

So, I held up a mirror and asked him to put on his thinking face. He looked back at me, shocked. "I had no idea I looked so angry," he said.

I encouraged him to tell his colleagues that he didn't realize how dramatic his facial expressions were because no one had ever mentioned them to him. It wasn't easy for him to share this, but he did it anyway. He suggested his colleagues ask him, "Is that your thinking face, or are you upset about something?" That way he would have a cue when his expressions sent the wrong message. This simple admission and request for accountability changed everything. People were more at ease with him and less concerned about what his face was unintentionally saying. He was also more willing to express his true thoughts because he felt more accepted by the team. It's not to say that he wasn't still difficult . . . he was. But we were able to make better decisions and keep meetings healthy and productive because of this conflict. Eventually, this employee ended up leaving the company; he had to modify himself too much, which was exhausting. The StoneAge culture and his work style were just not a good match.

Learning to manage conflict is fine and dandy, but what about those difficult people who drive you crazy? How can you minimize their impact on you while still benefiting from having different styles on your team? Here are my tips on handling yourself when you are ready to pull out your hair.

Put It into Practice:
How to Deal with Difficult People

First look within.

Always start with yourself. Is the person you find difficult truly the problem, or are you overreacting? Are you making assumptions or being too sensitive? While it's easy to blame the other person, you may have a role in the situation. Ask for feedback from a trusted coworker about how you're perceived when dealing with the problematic person. You may be surprised by what you learn.

See it from a different perspective.

Take a walk in the person's shoes. Try to think like them. What are their motivations and fears? What's their personality type, and how does that show up when they're stressed? If there is one thing you can do to improve your situation, try to see it from other people's perspectives. Doing so will give you the insight to flex your style to better match his, allowing you to have greater influence over the outcome.

Address issues directly.

The best way to resolve issues in the workplace is to deal with them directly. First, make sure you are not emotional; you will get the best results when you can be calm and collected. Ask questions first; always seek to understand before launching into your grievances. You may learn that your perception of the situation is incorrect, and you'll then be able to pivot if necessary. Explain why and how their behavior is negatively impacting you and others. Offer solutions to how they might be able to work more effectively within the team. Yes, it can be intimidating to approach a difficult person to give feedback, but nine times out of ten, you can progress by addressing the issue head-on. And don't forget to document your conversation. You can hope for the best, but many times, the employee will have to be terminated. If you don't have clear documentation of the discussion and agreed upon expectations, you set yourself and the company up for wrongful termination lawsuits.

Validate others.

When people feel unheard, some lash out, and sometimes all it takes to affect lousy behavior positively is to listen to the person and validate their feelings and concerns. According to the Society of Human Resources

Management (SHRM), "One of the main reasons employees engage in disruptive behaviors is because they don't feel they are being heard. When unacceptable behaviors appear, good managers will start to pay close attention to what is happening and not turn away from problems they'd rather ignore. Be sure to solicit the problematic employee's point of view. Just being heard can also be a factor in de-escalating negative behaviors before they get out of control." Start the conversation by saying, "These behaviors are creating issues for you and your coworkers. I'd like to understand what's going on from your perspective. Can you share with my what's going on?"

Pick your battles.

Some things are not worth being upset about or fighting for. Sometimes the best solution may be just to let go of your annoyance or frustration. How do you do this? Find something positive to appreciate about the person. Remind yourself that they are human and have hopes and fears, just like you. Smile to yourself and say *how fascinating* when they exhibit poor behavior. Choose to accept the person for who they are and where they are on this journey. Only choose battles worth fighting. Don't take it personally.

It's easy to make everything about you, and I'm here to tell you that 99 percent of the time, it's not. People are not purposefully trying to make your life miserable. Letting yourself become offended or defensive will only escalate the situation and prolong the conflict. Take a deep breath and remind yourself that this is really about whatever is going on with the other person.

• • •

Difficult people are challenging, but you will keep your cool, respond appropriately, and handle difficulty with grace and compassion if you practice these tips. There is always something to be gained in every experience, so ask yourself what you can learn and let the situation make you a better communicator, coworker, and person.

31

ACCEPT YOU WILL HAVE TO LET EMPLOYEES GO

Along with 99.9 percent of all other leaders on the planet, I hate firing people. It's the worst part of the job, but it's an inevitable part of leadership. According to SHRM, "Behavior that is not consistent with basic collegial and professional expectations can result in significant negative consequences to the organization and its people and can increase an organization's potential legal liability." Whether you must fire someone for underperformance, gossiping, bullying, insubordination, or general incivility, it's never easy. You are impacting their livelihood, and there is almost always organizational fall out, even when your employees agree with your decision to terminate employment.

One of my most insecure moments as a leader came when I had to fire an employee loved by our customers who had been with the company for twenty-one years. Although he got along well with the founders, he was disrespectful and insubordinate toward me. He would say one thing to my face, agree to a plan, and then do the exact opposite of what we had decided while trashing me behind my back. I tried everything to turn the relationship around, but it became clear that he wouldn't accept me as a leader no matter what I did. There was no option but to fire him, but I couldn't stop questioning myself. *Have I done everything in my power to turn it around? Am I a terrible leader? Will our customers leave if he leaves? Will I lose the respect of my employees if I fire him?* I lost countless nights of sleep and finally called him into my office. I told him that I was letting him go because he didn't keep his commitments and actively worked against me. He was disrespectful and insubordinate. He wasn't a good teammate, and I couldn't trust him. I was incredibly nervous, but I was determined to stand up for myself as a leader and a human. The good news is that none of the awful things I thought would happen came to fruition. He left quietly, and the sales team stepped up to fill the void. Within a month, it was like he was never there.

I have let many more people go since this fateful day. Running a growing, innovative, employee-owned company requires high performance. Some people have what it takes, and others don't. And sometimes, employees who were high performers in the earlier years can't scale their skills and talents with the company. Throughout the years, I have learned from each of them and have come up with ways to make letting people go easier on both the person and the manager.

Termination is never the ideal endpoint, and there are several approaches and strategies managers should employ before they get to the point of letting an employee go. First and foremost, termination should never be a surprise. If there are performance issues, they need to be addressed timely and directly and then documented appropriately. Every employee deserves to know where they stand, and avoiding difficult feedback doesn't allow for improvement, nor is it fair to them. When giving performance feedback, be clear on the issues and their impact on the individual, team, and company. Develop an improvement plan that holds the person accountable. Always provide follow-up feedback and check in regularly to make sure the employee is on track. Pro tip: Always document the conversation. I don't know how often I've seen a manager wind up in a difficult situation because they failed to document the discussions. I've made this mistake myself. It can be as simple as sending yourself an email with the details of the conversation and saving it in a folder or as severe as having the person sign a document that goes in their HR file. It depends on the severity of the issue and company policy.

Another thing I do is line up the second conversation during the first conversation. What does that mean? Simply line out the consequences of unchanged performance or behavior. It's much easier to say, "And if there isn't progress over the next thirty days, our next conversation will be about going on a performance improvement plan (PIP) or exiting the company," during the first difficult conversation than potentially surprising an employee with it down the road. Plus, the employee will understand the seriousness of the discussion. Leave little room for ambiguity; it will make it easier if you take the next step. There is a better chance the person can improve because they understand exactly what's expected going forward and the consequences of not improving performance.

Put It into Practice: What to Do When You Have to Fire Someone

Be direct, kind, and amicable.

No matter the situation or how upset you might be, you must manage your emotions and remember that we are all human beings with similar hopes, fears, and dreams. And no matter how difficult it is on you to let someone go, it's far more difficult being on the receiving end of termination. Don't draw out the conversation with pleasantries, and don't beat around the bush.

I always start the conversation by telling the person exactly what is about to happen. Why? Because as soon as you start hemming and hawing, the person begins to get the picture and goes into panic mode, trying to figure out what's happening. In fact, it's doubtful they will hear much of what you say after the words "we are terminating your employment today" come out of your mouth. Be direct and keep it simple by saying something like this, "Today's conversation is going to be difficult. After much discussion, we've decided that the best path forward for the company is to terminate your employment." Then pause. After the words sink in, share two of three reasons why you are terminating employment. Don't give a laundry list; it's demeaning and unproductive. Then say, "I am going to explain the process now, but I know you might have questions after you have time to process this. I'll be available to answer them for you, or if you are more comfortable, HR is prepared to help you." This approach is direct, calm, and kind.

If the employee gets emotional, be understanding. Acknowledge that it's hard to hear news like this and that it's okay to process it. If an employee gets combative, simply say that the conversation is over for now, and once they have had time to calm down, they are welcome to come back with questions or comments. No matter what they say, don't get defensive; instead, be kind and amicable, as it will help them more quickly move on.

Be prepared.

Try to anticipate how the conversation will go and be prepared for anything. Have all your termination documents ready and understand the process so you can explain it. Have two of three reasons why you are terminating employment and know what you will say if the employee tries to prolong the conversation. Know what you are going to do if the person cries or gets angry. Getting fired sucks, and you should be prepared for a reaction so you don't counter-react.

Be generous.

I err on the side of being overly generous when terminating employment. In fact, unless the firing is due to gross negligence or something over the top, we pay a severance. Why? Because we take full responsibility for a mishire. While paying a severance sometimes makes me cringe, it also is a small gesture that goes a long way. A few weeks' or months' pay can help the person land a bit softer. Most people live paycheck to paycheck, so a cushion won't put precarious finances at immediate risk. And it allows the person time to cool off. At StoneAge, we typically pay one to two weeks for every year of employment, but there is no hard rule. We keep our policy flexible, so we can decide based on the nature of the situation.

Don't leave the door open.

This goes hand in hand with my having the second conversation during the first piece of advice. It may be easier on you at the moment to let an emotional employee think there is a chance that you'll change your mind. But this is just kicking the can down the road. One of my favorite sayings is, "Hope in a relationship that's over is a horrible thing." Don't give the person hope if there isn't any. Be clear, direct, and don't leave the door open for further conversation.

Consider mindful transitions.

I read a fantastic *Harvard Business Review* article on what the author, Robert Glazer, CEO of Acceleration Partners (a global performance marketing agency), calls "mindful transitions."

Glazer says, "Mindful transition fosters an environment that encourages open communication where employees feel comfortable sharing their plans for the future—even if those plans involve leaving our company. It's intended to be a clear, thoughtful, and respectful approach to handling employee departures. Openly acknowledging that your company might not be the best fit for everyone long-term allows you to completely change your dialogue with your team members. When employees know they can openly and honestly discuss their career goals—and even professional unhappiness—everyone is enabled to amicably discuss the next steps toward mutually positive outcomes."

StoneAge has had a pay-to-quit policy for some time now, where we offer employees who are struggling or who aren't culturally aligned the choice of going on a PIP without severance if it doesn't work out or taking a pay-to-quit option immediately. This makes a choice easier—do the hard work of turning things around or leave with a cushion to help close the gap while searching for a new job. While not everyone is offered a pay-to-quit option, it has proven to be well received, and a successful mechanism to help people who are not part of the company's future move on. I like what the mindful transition philosophy can bring—a more graceful and less disruptive way to exit the company. Exiting employees favor it because expectations are clear, and they have the power to choose whether to stay and meet expectations or leave on their own terms. It's better for the company because most everyone knows that the exiting employee had a choice in the matter.

• • •

Terminating someone's employment is traumatic for both you and the person you are letting go. While it's never easy, following these steps can leave you feeling confident that you handled it as well as you could. More importantly, following these steps can help the terminated employee leave with their dignity intact.

32

BUILD A PLATFORM AND AMPLIFY YOUR MESSAGE

In 2015, I began speaking and writing about employee ownership and being the kind of leader who inspires ownership thinking. I am passionate about creating a company that gives back to its employees and the world. I believe that leaders need to take a stand and amplify their message of good. My message of good is simple: create meaningful, dignified jobs that allow people to work with purpose. Compensate them well, offer flexibility, and share in the company's success. Be a leader who is worth following.

I started my blog after a long trail run on a cool fall day. I was pondering my purpose and thinking about how to become a better speaker. I remembered a line out of a random book I had read about going back to what you loved to do as an adolescent. I loved to write but stopped when I went to engineering school. The answer to my purpose question was crystal clear to me at that moment: start writing again. To amplify my message, I must have a message. To speak on my message, I must be known for being a thought leader. I needed to get busy.

As soon as I got home from the run, I sat in front of my computer and researched blogging websites. By the end of the weekend, I had built my website using a simple drop-and-drag website builder, and I was up and writing. The more I wrote, the more people noticed. After a year of blogging, I was asked to write for industry publications and then speak at various events. Now you are reading this book. This is how you amplify your message. Millions of people may not know me, but I am impacting those I reach, and that's what matters. I believe in my heart that as I keep practicing, putting my words of equity, dignity, and strong leadership out into the world, my message will continue to be amplified.

The more I wrote, the more aware I became of my impact. I would share an article on LinkedIn or post something interesting StoneAge was doing around innovation or employee ownership, and people would send me direct messages saying how much a post resonated with them. So, I started posting more and more on LinkedIn. One day, someone said to me, "I love the brand you are building on social media," and I was shocked. I wasn't intentionally building my brand, but as I stepped back, I could see that's exactly what I was doing. I realized that sharing my leadership journey and philosophy would also build StoneAge's already powerful social media platform. So, I decided to go for it.

As I began building my brand on LinkedIn, I was a bit gun shy. My gut told me that my message of striving for exceptional leadership through vulnerability and connection would resonate. I believed wholeheartedly that promoting employee ownership to create employee engagement, well-being, and wealth creation was worthy of promotion. But still, *What would people think? Would my employees appreciate it? Would my industry accept it? Would people question what I was doing?* Then I read a 2019 "Connected Leadership" study by the Brunswick Group. The study surveyed 2,047 full- and part-time US workers of companies with more than 1,000 employees. It found that 65 percent of the participants said that it's important for their CEO to actively communicate about their company online. And it's a great recruitment tool; 60 percent of respondents said they would check executive social media accounts before accepting a job offer.

This study was all it took to convince me. I started out focusing on building the StoneAge brand. I shared posts that our marketing team put out and commented on customer posts. Then I began posting about employee ownership. I promoted all the amazing ways we took care of our customers and employees, telling our story and promoting the intertwinement of the employee and customer experience. The results were fantastic; we had more engagement across LinkedIn and a positive response to our brand.

Then I created a podcast, *Industrial Theory*, intending to give people in the industry a platform to tell their stories. It was very well received, creating a fun way to look at the global industry. I began receiving requests from leaders outside the industrial cleaning industry to come on the show, but I wanted to keep *Industrial Theory* focused. Wanting to build off the show's success, I created *Reflect Forward: Conversations on Leadership*, my leadership podcast. Having blogged for a few years, I revamped my website and created a fresh image and brand consistency. Then I started posting my thoughts, blogs, podcasts, and videos and articles that aligned with my values and vision. The results were outstanding.

And the proof is in the pudding. One day, I received this email from one of my employees.

Hi Kerry,

I was in Washington, DC, and New York City this past week, touring colleges with my daughter. She forgot her mask, so I loaned her the one I got from StoneAge with the little logo in the corner. We were touring Georgetown, and a man next to her, who was from Michigan, looked at her mask and said to her, "StoneAge? Is that the StoneAge with Kerry Siggins?" and she said, "Yes." He then proceeded to go on and on about StoneAge, and he knew all these things about the company and you personally from your blog, podcasts, and LinkedIn posts. He talked about how we are employee-owned and the Own It Mindset. He said you were inspirational, and your message resonated far and wide. He was an engineer who worked for General Motors and now does consulting, but he was a big fan of yours. It was kind of cool being so far away and meeting a total stranger and having him understand our company and you and what you both stand for in the engineering industry in general. I thought this was incredible, and I felt inspired to be a part of it. Anyways, I wanted to share this story with you.

What more can you ask for? This note confirms that the time and effort I put into creating and amplifying my platform is working. If you want to make an impact, you must do the work. It may be uncomfortable building a platform such as this, but it's worth it—and imperative—if you want to change the world. And you know how I feel about this—leaders need to step up and tackle the challenges that have plagued us and lay ahead of us. Waiting for someone else to do it simply doesn't work.

Put It into Practice:
How to Build a Platform
and Amplify Your Message

Identify your passion.

To be a thought leader, you need to develop your expertise and focus on making a difference. It needs to be authentic and from the heart; therefore, your platform should reflect your passion. You must be willing to tell stories and create connections so people care, and you'll tell better stories when you deeply believe in and care about your message. To help identify your passion, ask yourself these questions:

What brings me the most joy? What do I want to be known for, and does this align with what brings me the most joy? What do I enjoy talking about most and why? What would it look like to make a big impact on my audience? How will I feel if I became an influencer in this space?

Then, ask yourself these questions to refine your message: *What do I want to share with the world? What tone do I want to use? How do I want to share it? What are the main points of my message? How do I want people to feel when they read or listen to my message?*

Get involved.

Getting involved in organizations where your passions lie is the foundation to amplifying your message. By being involved, you have a seat at the table, shaping the ways others think and learning how others view the world. If you want to have influence, you must build your reputation as a thought leader and a person who puts in the time and effort to advance the movement. It also helps you build your brand.

Build your personal brand.

To amplify your message, you need to have a brand that others recognize. When people think about personal brand building, they often think of influencers like the Kardashians and are turned off. Whether we acknowledge it or not, we all have a personal brand, so why not be intentional about building your brand? Here are simple ways to create your message and expand your reach:

Step 1: Identify what you want to be known for; this is the foundation for your brand. In my case, I want to be known as a thought leader in business and leadership, particularly building an employee-owned company that creates wealth for its employees and closes the income inequality gap.

Step 2: Consider your audience. Who do you want to reach and why? Be specific; the broader your audience, the harder it is to connect with them. It's better to start small, build a community, and then expand your reach. Why? Because if you create a tight-knit, loyal following, they will help you amplify your message. If you start too broad, you might water down your message and get lost in the noise of the millions of others trying to amplify their messages.

Step 3: Develop your message. What is the tone you want to take and why? What will resonate with your audience? People love stories and connect deeper on shared experiences. What stories do you want to tell, and how will you tell them? Be authentic.

Step 4: Get started and be consistent. The only way to build a brand is to put your brand out there for the world to see. Develop a plan to build your brand and amplify your message. And be consistent. The more people see your brand, the more they will recognize it.

Step 5: Get professional headshots and photos that represent your personality. I recommend booking a photoshoot where you take multiple types of shots so you can use them across multiple platforms.

Use your voice.

You must use your words and refine your message if you want to amplify it. Write articles, speak at events, contribute to your industry association's publications, book interviews, reach out to podcast hosts, and ask to go on their shows. There are so many avenues to amplify your message, but you have to use them. And using them well means you must put effort into the words you write and speak. Consider hiring a speaking coach; I hired one recently, and the experience has been a game-changer. She has helped me refine my storytelling skills, taught me how to use voice inflection to generate emotion, and showed me how to create different versions of my message for different audiences. Another pro tip: use Grammarly when writing. While the software is not perfect, it can help turn mediocre writing into decent writing.

Employ smart social media.

Being active on social media is a must when you want to amplify your message, even if you hate social media. I am not a fan of many platforms, but they are an excellent way to amplify your message. Movements have been started on Twitter. Influencers have changed the way we think on Instagram. A vision can inspire followers on LinkedIn. You can amplify your brand and your message if you use social media intelligently. You can hire many firms to help you with this, but I don't use them. No one can replicate my message, tone, and vision, and I never want to come across as inauthentic. It takes a bit of time to create good content, but it's so worth doing on your own—at least while you are getting started. I use a simple social media post manager to create posts in advance and push them to all the platforms I engage with.

Choose a platform.

Each social media platform has its uses, and choosing one depends on what you want to achieve with your message. LinkedIn is suitable for establishing yourself as a thought leader. Twitter is good for announcements and updates—it's easy to use and quick to create content. Building a Twitter following is a good option if you are short on time. Instagram is a visual content platform, and it's a good choice if you are tech-savvy, have a brand that appeals to IG users, can generate enough visual content (e.g., images, videos), and don't intend to share a lot of links (i.e., to articles or the company website). I like IG because it's more personal; I share less business content and more "get to know me as a person" content on IG. Meta is good if you want to reach an older audience. You can also easily share content across platforms such as Instagram. But Meta is noisy, and if you have a business page, you must pay to play, boosting your posts so more people see them. TikTok and YouTube are great for video content and are a must-use if you want to connect with Gen Zers.

Create consistent and creative content.

Consistency is important, whether you post on social media, speak at industry events, or write blogs and articles. A flurry of activity followed by a period of inactivity won't create a community. So pick a cadence and stick with it. It's also essential to generate original, relevant, and creative content. Resharing is boring, and it doesn't build your reputation as a thought leader. Don't be afraid to showcase your style and personality; people want to connect with the real you, not some imaginary personality you are trying to create.

Interact with your community.

You can't build a community unless you communicate and interact with them. Reply to comments on posts, stay after a speaking gig to mingle with the audience, and answer questions. Engage in your tribe's social activity as well; building a platform and a brand worth following isn't one-sided.

Invest in public relations.

Hiring a PR firm can also help you build a platform and amplify your message. A good PR firm will help you refine your message and find avenues to speak and write. They have connections with media outlets that can publish articles or give you an interview. To find a firm that fits your style and needs, create a requirements document outlining what you want to achieve and why. What are the goals and outcomes you want to see? What does success look like? If possible, create a scorecard highlighting your most important requirements and use this as your selection tool when interviewing firms.

• • •

I'm often asked how I have the time to do all of this. First and foremost, making an impact is important to me, and it's easier to create time when purpose and passion drive you to do the work. I also use a social media scheduling tool to plan, design, and schedule my posts. I have prepared a few speeches, and I can customize them for the venue and audience. My marketing team created some basic assets I can reuse across multiple platforms. Yes, there is a learning curve associated with building your brand platform but like with all things, the more you practice, the easier it gets.

33

MATURE AS A LEADER

Motivational speaker and author Tony Robbins said, "Every problem is a gift—without problems, we would not grow." Throughout my journey as a CEO, I have learned a tremendous amount about what makes a good leader and what doesn't. And as I think about what separates good leaders from bad ones and how good leaders become great, one word keeps coming to mind: maturity.

Mature leadership combines experience and knowledge with self-awareness, self-control, and the ability to put others' needs before your own. Mature leaders forego the allure of short-term impulses for long-term gains. They understand themselves and are masters of their emotions, knowing how to adapt to what the situation requires. For example, sometimes you need to be a cool, calm, and collected leader, and sometimes you must show vulnerability and emotion. Mature leaders build strong teams because they understand that the collective is far more powerful than the individual.

All too often, we defer to leaders who blame others, deflect responsibility, put people down, and place personal interests in front of the collective. This type of leadership can create divisiveness, resentfulness, and fear—all of which are destructive to a culture and a company. We need solid, grounded leadership more than ever. We need mature leaders who can bring people together to resolve the biggest challenges we face in politics, business, and life across all corners of the globe. Business leaders need to step up to the plate to ignite powerful change that improves the lives of *all* of us, not just a few.

Through my experience and on my journey to leave a lasting impact, I've come to believe that we can all make a difference. We can tackle big problems and affect real change. Any leader can choose to put the good of the whole in front of the good of a few. But we have to make that choice. Maturing isn't easy.

I recall a meeting with StoneAge cofounder John Wolgamott after a strategic planning off-site many years ago. The executive management team and John, chairman of our board, traveled to Telluride, Colorado, for a two-day planning session. We were highly productive the first day and went out for a teambuilding dinner afterward. Telluride is a charming town, rich with mining history and bars that take you back to the Wild West. My team and I had a few too many drinks, and with inhibitions removed, the jokes started flying, many of which were inappropriate. The next day, we were sluggish, and several people were hungover. We got through day two of planning, but it was lackluster and painful. Back in the office the next day, John called me into his office and shared that he was surprised at the team's behavior. He felt we didn't show up as a professional team taking planning seriously. John was disappointed in the language and the drinking. "I quite honestly expect more from you," he said.

John was right, and I was ashamed. Instead of leading by example, I joined in the fun. I let the team down, disappointed him, and even more so, myself. I vowed never to let it happen again. We can have fun as a team *and* stay in control. And it was up to me to set the tone and lead by example.

Emotional management is also an important part of maturing as a leader. Early in my career, I would talk passionately about my opinions on all sorts of matters, and I wasn't always aware of how raising my voice affected the team. Every year, I asked my team for candid feedback and one year, they made it clear that my passion sometimes stifled communication. They collectively said, "You're not always aware of the impact you have on others. Your words matter, and when you get amped up, you can be intimidating."

Every time you lose your temper, raise your voice, or act in a way that intimidates people, you create small chunks of damage in your relationships. Your employees are wondering, *What's next?* They fear how your unpredictability will affect their jobs. That's why I embrace my mantra of "cool, calm, and collected." I don't want to react; instead, I want to lead as a level-headed leader who remains calm under pressure. I want to respond thoughtfully and help the situation rather than worsen it.

Maturing happens over time, but you can also initiate the maturing process. You can be proactive by slowing down and thinking before reacting. I recommend adopting a mantra that helps you keep your cool in high stress situations, like my "cool, calm, and collected." Maturing occurs when you choose your words wisely instead of blurting out your thoughts. Cultivating self-awareness will also help you mature more quickly. Adopting the ownership mindset will also help you mature more quickly.

Put It into Practice:
What Mature Leaders Do Differently

Lead by example.

Mature leaders know that all eyes are on them. They lead steadily, keeping everyone focused on the vision, mission, and culture. How they show up sets the tone, and they carefully cultivate team and company behaviors and norms, not by the words they use but by their actions.

Cultivate patience while pursuing a strategic vision.

Mature leaders know the importance of having a clear strategic vision and can withstand the pressure of "short-term" thinking. Execution takes discipline and time. Jeff Bezos summed it up well in his 2006 letter to shareholders: "Planting seeds that will grow into meaningful new businesses takes some discipline, a bit of patience and a nurturing culture."

Care about the details.

While avoiding unimportant minutia is critical, the best leaders understand that details matter. Why? Because they care about execution—execution is in the details, and it's also where vital insights and ideas come from. Great leaders don't sweat the small stuff, but they are very much in tune.

Build a great team.

No leader creates success alone; it takes teamwork, cooperation, and mutual trust. A mature leader looks at the world through the lens of "us" instead of "me." They spend time developing the people across the organization, helping strengthen the team at all levels so the company can operate seamlessly.

Address conflict effectively.

Mature leaders seek to understand before reacting to conflict, identifying differing perspectives and motives. They address difficult situations directly and rationally, looking for ways to resolve problems collaboratively. They approach disagreement with the knowledge that people are messy, allowing them to be both compassionate and firm in resolve.

Manage your emotions.

Many people confuse emotional management with emotional suppression; they are not the same things. Pretending like your emotions don't exist will create more problems in the long run. Instead, aim to manage your emotions by first identifying your feelings and why. Putting a label on them will help you understand them, which allows you to move through them. After you've named the emotions, tell yourself a different story. How can you channel your anger or sadness into something positive? Then do something that boosts your mood, like going for a walk, listening to your favorite music, or expressing gratitude and appreciation for someone else. Mature leaders don't let their emotions rule them; they identify, process, and move through them with grace and self-compassion.

Be a great listener.

The very best leaders are masters at asking questions and listening to what's being said, and, more importantly, what's not being said. They actively seek feedback and are genuinely interested in what people share with them. Great leaders are mindful of people's fear of speaking up and break down barriers by being thoughtful, active listeners.

Give credit to others.

Giving credit where credit is due strengthens bonds with employees and creates a culture where people know their hard work will be acknowledged and rewarded. Mature leaders never take credit for the company, departmental, or team wins; instead, they go out of their way to showcase their teammates' efforts and show appreciation for a job well done.

Admit your mistakes.

Great leaders understand that admitting mistakes is not a sign of weakness but strength and maturity. They always take responsibility for their screw-ups and can laugh at themselves, and this helps them build an organization where taking risks and making mistakes is accepted, even encouraged.

• • •

Leadership is a journey with no "final" destination. Learning, adapting, and improving should be lifelong efforts. No matter how successful you become, stay humble, curious, and control your words and emotions; doing so will allow you to mature into the best version of yourself and become an inspiring leader worthy of followership.

CONCLUSION

Being a leader is tough, and being an exceptional one is even tougher. Juggling multiple priorities, developing your people, growing your company, and handling the curveballs thrown at you can make you feel like you can never do enough. And the pressure to deliver—the pressure to perform—can be overwhelming. All eyes are on you, and you wonder how you can keep doing it all.

You are not alone. I get how hard it is to lead well, and I have succumbed to burnout due to constant pressure. I have driven myself and my team crazy, made huge mistakes, pushed past what I thought I was capable of, and came out the other side a stronger and better-respected leader. My passion and purpose are to help other leaders do the same.

I hope this book inspired you to be an exceptional leader who embraces the ownership mindset. I hope I have shown you that it's possible to build upon your past experiences, decisions, mistakes, and actions to transform yourself into the leader you know you can be. Your past got you to where you are now, and if it's serving you well, building upon it will help you take your life to the next level. If you don't like where you are, your past doesn't have to define you as a person or define where you are going, but you can only change it if you reflect on what is going well, what isn't going well, and decide what you want your life to look like going forward. You must own everything. You must reflect forward to be a better leader.

What does it mean to reflect forward? It's the ability to learn from your past and present, using your experience to create a forward trajectory.

I'll leave you three ways to reflect forward.

Show Up

The first step of reflecting forward is showing up. It may seem obvious but it's not easy for many. "Showing up" means being vulnerable, humble, and accountable. It means committing to do the hard work of looking at yourself to make necessary changes in your life to be a better person and leader. It means being honest with yourself while still loving yourself. Showing up requires fortitude and longevity. You can't show up one day a week and expect to transform your leadership style and impactfulness. Showing up is a daily practice, even if it means you need to unplug to rest and recharge so you can come back stronger.

Dig Deep

As Woody Allen famously said, "showing up is 80 percent of life." While I agree that showing up is incredibly important to being an exceptional leader, Thomas Edison's quote, "Genius is 1 percent inspiration, 99 percent perspiration," resonates with me a bit more. The only way to be a successful leader is to make a meaningful impact on their employees, industries, communities, and the world. One must do the hard work of learning, making mistakes, and ultimately transforming. Digging deep takes effort, transparency, discipline, resiliency, and self-leadership. It will require you to ask for help and feedback.

Make an Impact

To be the kind of leader worth following, your purpose and passion must intersect with your vision and plan to execute. You must be an effective connector, communicator, and problem solver. You must understand how to develop people to do their best work. You must be able to build a team, a company, and a community. And finally, you must find the best platform to advance your cause, whether through brand building, impacting social change, policy-shaping, or simply creating a culture where people thrive, which has a profound ripple effect.

• • •

Go out and make the world better by embracing your flaws, owning your actions, and developing yourself and your team. Exhibit the ownership mindset. The world needs you.

APPENDIX

StoneAge's Executive Operating Principles

Our mission as an executive management team

To build a better company. We work collaboratively to make the lives of each other, our teams, and our customers better.

Our purpose as an executive management team

- Create a vision for the company and tie it to the work we do.
- Determine the strategy to achieve that vision and propel the company forward.
- We understand the employee experience and customer experience are intertwined, and we work to create a customer- and employee-centric organization.
- Establish high-performance standards and hold ourselves and teams accountable.
- Set clear priorities and create measurable goals to track progress.

- Focus our teams on high-impact activities by communicating expectations and responsibilities.
- Ensure collaboration and alignment.
- Develop our employees and create engagement and a sense of purpose.
- To create an inclusive and equitable workplace where people are compensated well and treated with dignity and respect. We know every person's name in the company.
- Model the Own It Mindset: be a great teammate, practice self-leadership, and deliver on the StoneAge Assurance Promise.
- Model what a high-functioning, high-performing team looks like, leveraging unique and complementary talents that individuals bring to the team.

How we work together

- We help each other build strong teams that work together well.
- We frequently communicate, openly share information, and accept input from all stakeholders that lead to positive outcomes.
- We come to meetings prepared, and we actively participate.
- We determine the next steps, commitments, and communication plan after every meeting.
- We keep our commitments, both to the work we are doing and how we communicate and treat each other, and we hold each other accountable to our commitments.
- We keep it real with each other: we handle issues proactively and directly (no triangulation, no talking behind each other's backs). We assume good intentions and always work toward a positive outcome.
- We address problems head-on—no sweeping issues under the rug.

- We act like executives and represent our departments with integrity, honesty, and strong leadership.
- We have fun together and make an effort to get to know each other better (both in a group setting and one-on-one).

How we show up as leaders of the company

StoneAge's Leadership Principles

Leaders at StoneAge positively impact the lives of our employees and customers by solving problems and doing great work. Impact is only possible when we embody a proactive and positive leadership mindset. Leadership matters. Our leadership principles guide our decision-making, our mindset, and our culture. In addition to embodying the Own It Mindset, leaders at StoneAge share these attributes.

- Understand the importance of a positive mindset; be optimistic and helpful and have fun.
- Be willing to have difficult conversations; everyone deserves honest feedback.
- Build trust, be inclusive, and make it safe for all employees to speak up.
- Be transparent and always share the "why" behind decisions.
- Build engaged teams. Encourage personal growth and well-being.
- Continually raise the bar on performance.
- Create the vision, share intent, and communicate the significance.
- Bust silos; facilitate discussion and feedback and resolve conflict.
- Solve problems through collaboration and teamwork.
- Effectively use change management tools.
- Effectively manage complexity.

- Demonstrate competency, honesty, and approachability.
- Be responsible for understanding and contributing toward the entire strategic plan, not just your portion.

If done well, what does it mean for you?

It means success as an individual and team, greater overall well-being due to contributing to and being part of a healthy team that solves problems and gets things done, opportunities for growth and greater compensation (new projects, responsibilities, promotions), and recognition for success of the company.

If done well, what does this mean for the company?

It means more engaged culture, healthier teams, loyal and satisfied customers, stronger brand recognition, revenue and profit growth, new market opportunities, increased benefits for all (profit sharing, compensation, ESOP).

ACKNOWLEDGMENTS

I would like to first and foremost acknowledge my mother, Sue Petranek, for encouraging me to find my voice, spending countless hours editing my writing, and loving me unconditionally, especially in my darkest moments. Without you, I wouldn't be the writer, leader, mother, and human I am today. I love you. I would also like to acknowledge my supportive, funny, and brutally honest husband, Ryan Siggins; you keep me grounded, and I love you for always supporting and believing in me. And Jack Siggins, I can't even imagine my life without you. You are a remarkable human, and I am honored to be your mom. Thanks for letting me write my book on Saturdays while you skied.

Where do I even begin when it comes to my colleagues at StoneAge? I know! With John Wolgamott and Jerry Zink. Thank you for taking a risk on me all those years ago and putting up with me as I figured out how to be a leader. I have such respect for you both; you are the most generous people I have ever met. Thank you to my team at StoneAge—past, current, and future. I learn from you every day, and it takes my breath away watching you embrace the Own It Mindset to make it your own. We are a remarkable team doing remarkable things. Thank you for your trust and belief in me. And for forgiving me when I royally screw up. I'd also like to acknowledge my board of directors; without you, I wouldn't be the CEO I am today. Thank you for your support, feedback, and friendship.

I want to thank my publisher, Amplify Publishing, for helping me through the process of publishing my first book, especially Brandon Coward. Thank you for your never-ending patience with me! I would also like to thank Sara Stibitz and my fellow book-writing cohorts. Without you, I would never have finished this book. I also want to acknowledge my editor, Rebecca Andersen, for helping me turn my rough draft into something worth reading. I learned so much from you.

I want to thank the three coaches who have helped me be a better leader and CEO. Barbara Gormally—your wisdom and insight are magical. You helped me understand myself, and I am forever grateful to you. Ginger Jenks—your practical and direct style helped me address issues head-on, and your advice on dealing with employee issues sticks with me today. And finally, Chris Larkins—words cannot express how much you've changed my life. You help me organize my chaos, and there's no one I would rather have by my side as we build StoneAge into a billion-dollar company. Thanks for encouraging me to go big.

Joe Phillips, thank you for everything you did for me when I was a horrible person. I don't know if I would be alive if it weren't for your love, advice, and help. And to my brother, Eric Petranek, I love you, buddy. I still regret all those baby taps when we were teenagers. Samantha Cervantes, Allison Barr, Carrie Grant, Catie Bird, Betsy Fitzpatrick, Lily Wissing, and Carol Siggins, I appreciate our friendship over the years. I am forever grateful to have such strong, creative, funny, and inspiring women in my life.

I am an avid reader and appreciate many inspiring writers who have shared their ideas, wisdom, humor, and lessons learned with me through the written word. I can't list all the authors who have influenced me here, but I want to acknowledge the tremendous amount of good writing on this planet. Reading and writing make us uniquely human. I can't imagine my life without books or without writing, and I am honored to be one of you now.

ABOUT THE AUTHOR

Kerry Siggins is the CEO of StoneAge, a leading manufacturer of industrial cleaning equipment and one of *Outside* magazine's top 100 companies to work for. In 2021, she was honored by *Industry Era* magazine as one of its Top 10 Most Influential CEOs, and in 2017 she was a finalist for Colorado's CEO of the Year. She sits on the boards of several companies and is a member of the Young Presidents' Organization (YPO). She is regularly invited to deliver keynote speeches on several business and leadership topics, including how to create employee-centric cultures in which it's safe to speak up and show up as your whole self. She is an active blogger and contributor to *Forbes*, *Entrepreneur*, *Authority* magazine, and *BIC* magazine, and hosts several podcasts, including the popular *Reflect Forward*.